AN
ORIGIN
LIKE
WATER

W. W. NORTON & COMPANY / NEW YORK / LONDON

AN
ORIGIN
LIKE
WATER

COLLECTED POEMS 1967–1987

EAVAN BOLAND

Special acknowledgment is made to Carcanet Press.

The text of this book is composed in Electra
with the display set in Bernhard Modern
Composition by Crane Typesetting Service, Inc.
Manufacturing by The Courier Companies, Inc.
Book design by JAM DESIGN

Library of Congress Cataloging-in-Publication Data

Boland, Eavan.
    An origin like water : collected poems, 1967–1987 / Eavan Boland.
        p.   cm.
    Includes index.
    1. Ireland—Poetry.   I. Title.
PR6052.O35O75   1996
821'.914—dc20   95–19645

ISBN 0-393-03852-1

W. W. Norton & Company, Inc., 500 Fifth Avenue, New York, N.Y. 10110
W. W. Norton & Company Ltd., 10 Coptic Street, London WC1A 1PU

1 2 3 4 5 6 7 8 9 0

For my daughters,
Sarah and Eavan Frances

Contents

Preface

The first poems here were written when I was nineteen. Altogether, this book consists of five collections, published over twenty years, from *New Territory* in 1967 to *The Journey* in 1987. I have revised some poems, but not many. I have tried to leave intact the untidy and telling shape which is the truth of any poet's work, and I have avoided as much as I could the temptation to make any of it look more achieved and symmetrical than it was.

In a certain sense, I began in a city and a poetic world where the choices and assumptions were near to those of a nineteenth-century poet. The formal poem was respected. The wit of the stanza was admired more than its drama. Most importantly, the poet's life—in the small circle I knew and even beyond it in the culture—was exalted in ways that were poignant and suspect at the same time.

In my first collection, published when I was twenty-two years of age, those features of my environment showed up in poems that described a safe and well-lighted circle, that struggled for skill and avoided risk. Looking back at them now, I can see myself as I was then trying to get cadences right and counting out stresses on a table. The poems are the visible evidence. What is not visible is the growing confusion and anxiety I felt, my inability to be sure that I would continue to be a poet when I left the lighted circle and moved out into the shadow of what I had learned to think of as an ordinary life—that is, a life not to be found in the approved versions I had encountered. Above all I had no clear sense of how my womanhood could connect with my life as a poet, or what claims each would make on the other.

These poems are a record of the claims. By and large, I have left them as they are, with their failures, their awkwardness, because although the connection was often flawed and painful, it remains central: The truth is that I came to know history as a woman and a poet when I apparently left the site of it. I came to know my country when I went to live at its margin. I grew to understand the Irish poetic tradition only when I went into exile within it.

These are small paradoxes. They are reflected here in the poems I began to write when I left an eloquent literary city and went to live in a suburb only four miles from the city's center in actual distance, but unmapped and unvisited in any literary sense I knew. Once I began to live my own life—a life with a husband, a home, and small children—I could see firsthand how remote it was from the life of the poet as I had understood it. I began to realize that a subtle oppression could result from this fracture between the instinctive but unexpressed life I lived every day and the expressive poetic manners I had inherited that might easily—as manners often do—render it merely as decorum. I was grateful for the instruction of an historic poetic culture and I still relished craft and hard work. But increasingly I came to regard each poem not as a series of technical strategies, but as a forceful engagement between a life and a language.

It was never predictable. I could never count on the outcome. The language remained partially inherited: resistant and engrossing. But the life at least was wholly mine. It took place in a house, in a garden, with a child in my arms, on summer afternoons, in winter dusks, and with eventual confidence that however formidable a poetic tradition might be, however assured its inherited language, its ethical survival still depended on the allowance it provided for a single life to make—in the ironic and historic sense—a new name for itself and commend it to all the old ones.

I am not suggesting that this assurance is clearly present in these poems. It could not be. It is retrospective: I only found it by writing them. In the earliest work here I was often too young, too puzzled, too clumsy as a technician to compose my intuitions into forms and therefore trapped them into patterns. Even later, when I found my voice, I was still capable of drowning it out with a finished poem. But occasionally—and these are the poems I am glad to have included here—the life beckoned to the language and the language followed.

EAVAN BOLAND
Dublin 1995

from
New Territory
1967

Athene's Song

From my father's head I sprung
Goddess of the war, created
Partisan and soldiers' physic,
My symbols boast and brazen gong,
Until I made in Athens wood
Upon my knees a new music.

When I played my pipe of bone,
Robbed and whittled from a stag,
Every bird became a lover,
Every lover to its tone
Found the truth of song and brag.
Fish sprung in the full river.

Peace became the toy of power
When other noises broke my sleep.
Like dreams I saw the hot ranks
And heroes in another flower
Than any there. I dropped my pipe
Remembering their shouts, their thanks.

Beside the water, lost and mute,
Lies my pipe and, like my mind,
Remains unknown, remains unknown.
And in some hollow, taking part
With my heart against my hand,
Holds its peace and holds its own.

From the Painting *Back from Market* by Chardin

Dressed in the colors of a country day—
Gray-blue, blue-gray, the white of seagulls' bodies—
Chardin's peasant woman
Is to be found at all times in her short delay
Of dreams, her eyes mixed
Between love and market, empty flagons of wine
At her feet, bread under her arm. He has fixed
Her limbs in color and her heart in line.

In her right hand the hindlegs of a hare
Peep from a cloth sack. Through the door
Another woman moves
In painted daylight. Nothing in this bare
Closet has been lost
Or changed. I think of what great art removes:
Hazard and death. The future and the past.
A woman's secret history and her loves—

And even the dawn market from whose bargaining
She has just come back, where men and women
Congregate and go
Among the produce, learning to live from morning
To next day, linked
By a common impulse to survive although
In surging light they are single and distinct
Like birds in the accumulating snow.

New Territory

Several things announced the fact to us:
The captain's Spanish tears
Falling like doubloons in the headstrong light
And then of course the fuss—
The crew jostling and interspersing cheers
With wagers. Overnight
As we went down to our cabins, nursing the last
Of the grog, talking as usual of conquest,
Land hove into sight.

Frail compasses and trenchant constellations
Brought us as far as this.
And now air and water, fire and earth
Stand at their given stations
Out there and are ready to replace
This single desperate width
Of ocean.
                        Why do we hesitate?

                                                Water and air
And fire and earth, and therefore life, are here.
And therefore death.

Out of the dark man comes to life and into it
He goes and loves and dies
(His element being the dark and not the light of day)
So the ambitious wit
Of poets and exploring ships have been his eyes—
Riding the dark for joy—
And so Isaiah of the sacred text is eagle-eyed because
By peering down the unlit centuries
He glimpsed the holy boy.

After the Irish of Aodghan O'Rathaille

Without flocks or cattle or the curved horns
Of cattle, in a drenching night without sleep
My five wits on the famous uproar
Oft the waves, toss like ships,
And I cry for boyhood, long before
Winkle and dogfish had defiled my lips.

O if he lived the prince who sheltered me,
And his company who gave me entry
On the river of the Laune,
Whose royalty stood sentry
Over intricate harbors, I and my own
Would not be desolate in Diarmuid's country.

Fierce McCarthy Mor whose friends were welcome,
McCarthy of the Lee, a slave of late,
McCarthy of Kanturk whose blood
Has dried underfoot:
Of all my princes not a single word—
Irrevocable silence ails my heart.

My heart shrinks in me, my heart ails
That every hawk and royal hawk is lost.
From Cashel to the far sea
Their birthright is dispersed
Far and near, night and day, by robbery
And ransack, every town oppressed.

Take warning wave, take warning crown of the sea,
I O'Rathaille—witless from your discords—
Were Spanish sails again afloat
And rescue on your tides
Would force this outcry down your wild throat,
Would make you swallow these Atlantic words.

The Flight of the Earls

Princes, it seems, are seldom wise.
Most of them fall for a woman's tears
Or else her laughter—think of Paris
Whose decision stretched to ten alarming years.
Nothing would suit
Until he'd brought
The kingdom down around his ears.

Now in the Middle Ages see
The legendary boy of king and queen:
A peacock of all chivalry
He dies at twenty on some battle-green
And ever since
The good Black Prince
Rides to the land of might-have-been.

Whether our own were foolish or wise
Hardly concerns us: death ran away with our chances
Of a meeting. Yet we strain our eyes
Hoping perhaps just one with his golden flounces
Has outwitted theft.
So are we left
Writing to headstones and forgotten princes.

A Cynic at Kilmainham Jail

There is nowhere that the gimlet twilight has not
Entered, not a thing indeed to see
But it is excellent abroad for ghosts:
A gaslamp in the dark seems to make sea
Water in the rising fog—maybe
For those imprisoned here this was a small
Consoling inland symbol—
how could their way be
Otherwise discovered back to the western seaboard?
How could they otherwise be free in prison
Who for more than forty years have been shot through
To their Atlantic hearts?
                                 But in this wizened
Autumn dark, no worship, mine or yours,
Can resurrect the sixteen minds. O those
Perhaps (Godspeed them) saw the guns with dual
Sight—seeing from one eye with the tears they chose
Themselves the magic, tragic town, the broken
Countryside, the huge ungenerous tribe
Of cowards and the one eye laughing saw
(God help them) growing from their own graves to jibe
At death, a better future, neither tear nor flaw.

Belfast vs. Dublin

Into this city of largesse
You carried clever discontent,
And now, the budget of your time here spent,
Let us not mince words: This is no less
Than halfway towards the end. Gathering
In a rag tied to a stick, all in confusion,
Dublin reverence and Belfast irony—
Now hoist with your confusion.

Cut by the throats before we spoke
One to another, yet we breast
The dour line of North and South, pressed
Into action by the clock. Here we renounce
All dividend except the brilliant quarrel
Of our towns: mine sports immoral
Courtiers in unholy waste, but your unwitty,
Secret love for it *is* Belfast city.

We have had time to talk and strongly
Disagree about the living out
Of life. There was no need to shout.
Rightly or else quite wrongly
We have run out of time, if not of talk.
Let us then cavalierly fork
Our ways since we, and all unknown,
Have called into question one another's own.

Yeats in Civil War

In middle age you exchanged the sandals
Of a pilgrim for a Norman keep
in Galway. Civil war started. Vandals
Sacked your country, made off with your sleep.

Somehow you arranged your escape
Aboard a spirit ship which every day
Hoisted sail out of fire and rape.
On that ship your mind was stowaway.

The sun mounted on a wasted place.
But the wind at every door and turn
Blew the smell of honey in your face
Where there was none.
                      Whatever I may learn
You are its sum, struggling to survive—
A fantasy of honey your reprieve.

The Poets

They like all creatures, being made
For the shovel and worm,
Ransacked their perishable minds and found
Pattern and form
And with their own hands quarried from hard words
A figure in which secret things confide.

They are abroad. Their spirits like a pride
Of lions circulate.
Are desperate. Just as the jeweled beast,
That lion constellate,
Whose scenery is Betelgeuse and Mars,
Hunts without respite among fixed stars.

And they prevail. To his undoing every day
The essential sun
Proceeds, but only to accommodate
A tenant moon
And he remains until the very break
Of morning, absentee landlord of the dark.

Mirages

At various times strenuous sailing men
Claim to have seen creatures of myth
Scattering light at the furthest points of dawn—

Creatures too seldom seen to reward the patience
Of a night-watch, who provide no ready encore,
But, like the stars, revisit generations.

And kings riding to battle on the advice
Of their ambition have seen crosses burn
In the skylight of the winter solstice.

Reasonable men however hold aloof,
Doubting the gesture, speech and anecdote
Of those who touch the Grail and bring no proof—

Failing to recognize that in their fast
Ethereal way mirages are
This daylight world in summary and forecast.

So a prince, a fledgling still, and far
From coronation, kept at home,
Will draw his sword and murder empty air—

And should his father die and that death bring
Him majesty, his games have been his school,
His phantom war a forcing house of kings.

The Pilgrim

When the nest falls in winter, birds have flown
To distant lights and hospitality:
The pilgrim, with her childhood home a ruin,
Shares their fate and, like them, suddenly
Becomes a tenant of the wintry day.
Looking back, out of the nest of stone
As it tumbles, she can see her childhood
Flying away like an evicted bird.

Underground, although the ground is bare,
Summer is turning on its lights. Spruce
And larch and massive chestnut will appear
Above her head in leaf: Oedipus
Himself, cold and sightless, was aware
Of no more strife or drama at Colonus.
He became, when he could go no further,
Just an old man hoping for warm weather.

At journey's end, in the waters of a shrine,
No greater thing will meet her than the shock
Of her own human face, beheaded in
The holy pool. Steadily she must look
At this unshriven thing among the bells
And offerings and, for her penance, mark
How her aspiring days, like fallen angels,
Follow one another into the dark.

Migration

From August they embark on every wind
Managing with grace
This new necessity, widely determined
On a landing place.
Daredevil swallows, colored swifts go forth
Like some great festival removing south.

Cuckoo and operatic nightingale
Meeting like trains of thought
Concluding summer, in complete agreement, file
Towards the sea at night
And find at last their bright geometry
(Triumphant overland) is not seaworthy.

Sandpiper, finch and wren and goldencrest
Whose baffled
Movements start or finish summer now at last
Return, single and ruffled,
And raise their voices in a world of light
And choose their loves as though determined to forget:

As though upon their travels, as each bird
Fell down to die, the sea
Had opened, showing those above a graveyard
Without sanctity—
Birds and their masters, many beautiful,
Huddled together without name or burial.

Three Songs for a Legend

1. A Lullaby for Lir's Son

O nurse when I was a rascal boy
Bold February winds were snaffling gold
Out of the crocuses. There in grief
For the pretty, gaudy things I'd shout *Stop Thief!*
And you would whisper *Child, let be. Let be.*

Or else we'd come across a sapling tree
To discover frost sipping its new blood.
I'd join my arms around its perished wood
And weep and you would say *Now child, its place
Is in a crackling hearth, not your embrace.*

And one April morning that was filled
With mating tunes a nest of finches spilled,
Which slipped its flowering anchor in a gale.
I cupped one in my fingers. Dead. Small.
But late that night you came to me on tiptoe
And whispered *child, child, the winds must blow.*

2. The Malediction

Son of Lir as lonely are you now
As the leaf when lightning strikes the tree
And the bird when thunder breaks the bough.
Now is lost, as bird and leaf and tree,
Son of Lir your humanity.

Now the steady shoulders, the bright arms
You opened wide for battle and love's sake—
Encumbered to white wings by my charms—
Must beat the air and the air must break
With your human heart, your tender neck.

The seed of man is barren in this body!
The wit of man abandons this cursed brain!
The blood of man turns back and flows muddy
From this changing heart and this fair skin
Is ruffling in the feathers of a swan.

I take your youth under magic seizure.
Farewell the joy of summer in a field.
Farewell the simple seasons and their pleasure.
Farewell true gold and the silk worm's yield.
Son of Lir I banish you this world

To know the flinching cold of seas which spring
Forgets, whose branch is ice, whose flower is snow
And where the wild dead lie wintering
Forever.

3. Elegy for a Youth Changed to a Swan

Now the March woods will miss his step,
Finding out a way at spring's start
To break at once their bracken and their sleep,
And now have lost, robbed of their rightful part,
Some hawk a master's hand, some maid a heart.

Urchins of the sharp hawthorn, sparrows,
Spiders webbed in hedges, brown
Field mice, wheeled, sleeping in their furrows,
Spared by the plow and stout with corn—
These were familiars of Lir's son

No less than the stiff, aloof lily,
The oak and the hawk, the Moy salmon
On February mornings, unruly
With new life and the flushed rowan
Stooped with berries, October's paragon.

Sap of the green forest, like a sea,
Rise in the sycamore and rowan,
Rise in the wild plum and chestnut tree
Until the woods become a broad ocean
For my son in his wilderness, my swan,

That he may see breaking on his breast
And wings, not the waters of his exile,
Nor the pawn of the wind, the cold crest,
But branches of the white beam and the maple
And boughs of the almond and the laurel.

The King and the Troubadour

A troubadour once lost his king
    Who took a carved lute
And crossed the world and tuned its heart
    To hear it sing.

Starved, wasted, worn, lost—
    His lute his one courage—
He sang his youth to fumbling age,
    Fresh years to frost.

In bitter spells his king lay bound
    In bitter magic walled:
Within a cruel shape swelled
    Love no sound,

No sight, no troubadour searching
    Could set free. Fiercely
Came he singing finally
    My king, my king.

To the window the king's head
    Came. The troubadour
Dashed his lute on leaf and flower
    And fell dead.

The king at one glance,
    Seeing ransom ruined,
Majesty perplexed, pined
    In magic silence.

The rain of God gathering
    Surrounded the smashed lute,
Solving its fragmented heart
    Into spring.

The king who in a cruel husk
    Of charms became as tragic
Through monotonies of magic
    As the dusk,

Each minstrel spring was called and sent
    No horrid head, but came
Above the ground, a grassy atom
    Hearty as a giant.

Requiem for a Personal Friend

A striped philistine with quick
Sight, quiet paws, today—
In gorging on a feathered prey—
Filleted our garden's music.

Such robbery in such a mouthful.
Here rests, shoveled under simple
Vegetables, my good example—
Singing daily, daily faithful

No conceit and not contrary—
My best colleague, worst of all
Was half digested, his sweet whistle
Swallowed like a dictionary.

Little victim, song for song—
Who share a trade must share a threat—
So I write to cheat the cat
Who got your body, of my tongue.

The Winning of Etain

Etain twice a woman twice a queen
Possessed of two lives and one love.
Twice the loveliest woman ever seen.
For whom two kings made Ireland a red grave.
    This story tells the winning of Etain
    A second time by Aengus: how he strove
    To own his own. A tale of tears. Of lovers
    Lost to each other for a thousand years.

Aengus and Etain lived for each other's pleasure,
With gold for the head of Aengus as a king
And gold so intricate in Etain's hair
No one could guess if the light scattering
    Were a woman's beauty or a king's treasure.
    They lived for summer and to dance and sing.
    But they were doomed when Fergus, the black Druid,
    Followed their happiness with fatal hatred.

A summer's night Etain in Aengus's arms
Slept, her head challenging the moon,
Collecting more and more light from beams
Which flared on lovers who would not love again
    For a thousand years. All at once the charms
    Of Fergus took effect: Unlucky Etain,
    Warm in Aengus's arms where she lay,
    Lost her happiness, mislaid her joy.

Her cheeks, blanched with light, were charmed away.
Her long embracing arms convulsed. Her face
Shriveled. Quick and violent decay
Seized her limbs and her body's grace
    Changed from a queen into a dragonfly,
    Changed to enameled wings and scales in a space
    Of minutes. Then she flew in a glimmer
    Away to discover flowers of the summer.

Awakening, Aengus found instead of Etain
His arms as empty as a spring nest
Rifled by hawks and found his love gone—
No hand to kiss and for his head no breast.
>   From his window in a summer dawn
>   Bright as blood, idly he watched the haste
>   Of birds from branch to branch and below
>   A dragonfly sipping at the dew.

Morning danced on its back and decorated
Every scaly tone twice as bright
As hyacinths, above which it waited
Wings singing, a busy thief of light
>   And dew. A thousand insect colors scattered
>   From its body and were deftly caught
>   By summer flowers like another rain,
>   And Aengus in that moment cried, "Etain—

"My only love, changed to a brilliant toy
Of sorcery, for you I will compose
A bower of the four seasons and defy
Our new despair. Autumn, the year's close,
>   Summer and spring will tangle for your joy,
>   The frosty snowdrop twine with the rose,
>   And January buds with fringed grasses
>   Where you may stay under my jealous eyes."

At Aengus's command the thing was done.
Season followed season in his grief
And for each one a sweet, particular crown
Was stolen. Bough and petal, fruit and leaf,
>   Were interwoven for his spellbound queen
>   And flowered endlessly about his wife
>   Who hummed night and day about her many
>   Suitors, robbing each of dew and honey.

And night and day, Aengus stayed beside,
Asleep or waking, hawking or at rest,
He watched the fertile bower and his bride
Within, but thinking of her white breast,
>   Her human body in his arms, he cried
>   Bitterly above the bright twist

Of flowers, but his fast tears were human—
His love, an insect, drank them like the rain.

And still the Druid's hatred followed them
Redoubled now because they could devise
Happiness within destruction, a form
Of beauty flourishing within disguise.
    So he contrived darkness and a storm
    Of winds colliding on the fresh seas
    To separate the crocus from the rose
    And interrupt the dragonfly's repose.

Suddenly, as Aengus watched, the wind
Tore his green and intricate design
Apart, scattered flowers and unwound
Summer from spring, and wealthy autumn's vine
    From winter leaves. He flung his hand
    Among stems broken and a rain
    Of petals. But the wind swept them towards
    The sea where its strength was bred, like birds.

"O Etain my first love," Aengus cried,
"Stolen a second time, now who will build
A bower for you over the cold tide?
What blossoms of the country or the field
    What flower or fragrance can the sea provide?
    And where will you find dew in the salt
    Of the waves? I cast this wretched world behind
    And will not rest until my love is found!"

At his cry the better powers took pity
On him, loving him because his love
Had once set out to cheat the travesty
Of sorcery and triumphed, but could not save
    Etain twice. Invisibility
    Was their gift, exemption from the grave—
    As well they gave a thousand mortal years
    To Aengus and Etain, unlucky lovers.

Like a petal on the flowers sipped
By her on bright days at Aengus's side,
Etain fluttered while the north wind clipped

Her colored scales and the sea cried
    Beneath her. Once she struggled, wings trapped
    In the beak of a scavenger, but she escaped
    And tossed, a magic atom, on the surface
    Of the water, lost in the water's race.

Etain at last, baffled and long weary,
Was wildly buffeted, now on a snowy
Now on a stifling breeze, until clearly
A green and quiet shore began, whose dewy
    Grasses sprung out of the wind's way
    And there found flowers in hosts, scarlet and showy
    Rivals for her wings, petals to soothe
    Her misery and honey for her mouth.

And there she flew above a royal palace
Whose roof, involved and circled like a rose,
Bore mosaics like a clutch of crocuses
And marble whiter than the lily grows.
    No wonder then she searched for dew and spice
    Among its tiles, mistaking them for flowers
    And tumbled through a cranny, all unseen
    To splash in the bright wine of another queen.

And by that error found another womb,
Another spell of life, another shape
For the queen lifting up the same
Infested gold cup to her lip
    Swallowed insect, wine and all, while the fume
    Of the delicate fermented grape
    Disguised its tenant. But magic had its way
    And worked its charm, and swelled the queen's belly.

Mysteriously she came to be with child,
Another queen, wife of another king
And in another age. She grew heavy and mild.
Contented with the chance, never suspecting
    She was fertile from the wine defiled
    And not a king's embrace. And so in spring
    Was born human, from a magic womb,
    Etain into the world a second time.

And so she grew to girlhood cherishing
All captive things and grew to hate the forest
Because its horned boughs might be concealing
A bold antelope in charmed arrest.
          And wept on summer nights imagining
          The lion howling from his heaven, cased
          In stars; but never guessed from where her pity
          Sprung, from what unknown captivity.

Where a river rushed into the sea, on a ledge
Of stone, Etain would sit in the evening glow,
Her cheeks as fresh as berries from the hedge,
Her arms white as a single fall of snow,
          Her thighs like stems of a flower. And to the edge
          Of the water where outrivaled lilies grew
          On a summer night (in every detail the same
          As that on which he lost her) Aengus came.

Invisible he watched her silver comb,
Chased with gold, calm her golden hair.
Invisible, he brought to mind a time
When she had bound it up for him with fair
          Ornaments which he, when night came,
          Unbound again with all a lover's care,
          But in another royal life, of
          Which nothing remained only love.

"O world," cried Aengus, "I have found again
My only love restored to loveliness
For whom I interwove, to catch the sun,
A bower of every blossom, fruit and grass
          In each material, from every season
          When she was changed by a Druid's malice
          And watched her drink its dew and suck
          Its honey, and never realized our luck.

"How can I kiss those red forgetful lips
This unfamiliar hand, or take this body
Which has traveled through so many shapes
Of magic to my side? Can an unready
          Girl give back a woman? Can green pips
          Sweeten the tongue like fruit? Or seedy

Grain be wholesome wheat overnight?
And will I ever find again delight

Which I have searched for in a thousand years?
Invisible but none the less in pain
And none the less a creature of my tears
Crying at corners of the world 'Etain'
    Without an answer? And now for all my loss
    I must begin to woo my love again.
    No arms await me and no recognition
    Only the chance to win again what's mine."

Day by summer day Aengus stayed
Beside the cool lake and watched his love
Grow graceful as the forest deer which wade
And drink at dawn, and saw her beauty thrive
    And knew she fretted. "She will be a bride
    Before the winter. She for whom I wove
    A shelter out of flowers will shelter now
    In other arms, and I have lost my labor."

Out of the south one day a horseman rode,
His head the color of the harvest corn,
His cloak full, jeweled and embroidered,
A sword weighing at his side, a horn
    Curving at his shoulder. There he wooed
    Etain while Aengus watched, his heart torn
    In two, hearing his love say "Yes I will
    Give you love for love upon that hill."

Dawn broke after a fevered night
In cold waves, wide as the sea is deep,
Capsizing the half moon in tidal light,
But Aengus threw his rival into a sleep
    As blind as death and by the dreadful right
    Of love, disguised himself within that shape
    And climbed the hill alone and there appeared
    To Etain as the lover she desired.

All about them acorns and dried leaves
Lay close as gold and silver at a feast,
Friendly trees shaded them in groves

And the sun rising was their priest—
      And even by the hours, usual thieves
      Of love, they knew that their embrace was blessed.
      And Aengus wept, half for simple joy,
      Half to be within another body.

Knowing it as the necessary price
Of his possession, yet he felt despair
Because he spoke within another voice
And kissed with strange lips Etain's fair
      Lips. And knew that they were loving twice
      In two forms, yet with a single fire.
      "What would you say Etain if you should know
      I loved another woman long ago?"

"My only love," said Etain, "overhead
Autumn is decking out the chestnut tree
With embers. Our cheeks are pressed against dead
Flowers and we have been lovers in a chilly
      Womb of snow. But spring will fling a vivid
      Color on this tree and make ready
      The world and with a same difference
      The heart can love again and yet love once.

"Are buds less welcome to the April bough
Because they open where all others have?
Is snow less white, the wingspan of the crow
Less black because their purities survive
      From past to future and from then to now?
      And so is any love not every love?"
      And with her words Aengus came to rest
      At last and slept safely on her breast.

With many a trumpet, many a bell's mouth
Opened like a bird's under the sun,
Etain married Conor, King of the South,
Imagining him the lover who had lain
      With her, ignorant of the strange truth.
      But very soon discovered to her pain
      Her heart was cold, pressed beneath a weight
      Like ice while her love turned to hate.

Bitter words were woven into the stuff
Of disappointment. "How can I say," she cried,
"Where love has gone. I loved you well enough
That bold autumn morning on the hillside."
        Then Conor turned to her, his speech rough:
        "I slept that dawn as though I had been dead."
        And Etain's heart stirred, her tears
        Fell on the stiff frost of a thousand years.

The weather changed. Winter with its harsh
Colors became spring. Flowers grew.
A stilted crane waded in the marsh,
An argosy of summer fruits blew
        Inland on the winds, wild and fresh.
        Etain only was unstirred by the view
        Of the earth waking, but sat alone sewing
        Always at her window, always waiting.

Like January's rose to one of June
Her scarlet cheeks dwindled into white.
Her round flesh almost into bone,
The brilliance of her eye became a twilight.
        And as the green earth swelled great
        With child she sickened, separate and thin.

May came and the trees were stirred
By blossoms tumbling from their brief stations,
Wrapping the flamboyant earth in a shroud
Like snow, when Etain, sick with long patience
        Saw a figure like a far bird
        Enlarge at last and block the summer distance,
        And saw a horseman in a rich dress
        Drumming across the drawbridge of the palace.

And he was armoured in a suit of seasons:
Flowers of spring adorned his iron greaves;
The icy evergreen, the berry's poisons
Enameled his wintry visor. Flushed leaves
        Of autumn inflamed his breast like suns
        And summer was imprinted on his sleeves
        And what with berry, leaf, tree and flower
        He seemed no horseman but a human bower.

And where his lady's token should have been
A scarf of silk, marked in brilliant paints,
Flapped wildly to the wind's motion,
On which a dragonfly, seeming at once
    To light on every flower, had been drawn.
    And Etain from her window knew the prince
    Was Aengus. And ran to him and took his arm
    And mounting up, rode away with him.

I

from
The War Horse
1975

Dedication: The Other Woman and the Novelist

(FOR KEVIN)

I know you have a world I cannot share
Where a woman waits for you, beautiful,
Young no doubt, protected in your care
From stiffening and wrinkling, not mortal

Not shy of her own mirror. How can I rival
Her when like another wife she waits
To come into the pages of your novel,
Obediently, as if to your bed on nights

She is invited nor, as in your other life
I do, reminds you daily of the defeat
Of time nor, as does your other wife,
Binds you to the married state?

She is the other woman. I must share
You with her time and time again,
Book after book. Yet I am aware,
Love, that I may have the better bargain:

I imagine she has grown strange
To you among the syntax and the sentences
By which you distance her. And would exchange
Her speaking part for any of our silences.

The War Horse

This dry night, nothing unusual
About the clip, clop, casual

Iron of his shoes as he stamps death
Like a mint on the innocent coinage of earth.

I lift the window, watch the ambling feather
Of hock and fetlock, loosed from its daily tether

In the tinker camp on the Enniskerry Road,
Pass, his breath hissing, his snuffling head

Down. He is gone. No great harm is done.
Only a leaf of our laurel hedge is torn

Of distant interest like a maimed limb,
Only a rose which now will never climb

The stone of our house, expendable, a mere
Line of defense against him, a volunteer

You might say, only a crocus, its bulbous head
Blown from growth, one of the screamless dead.

But we, we are safe, our unformed fear
Of fierce commitment gone; why should we care

If a rose, a hedge, a crocus are uprooted
Like corpses, remote, crushed, mutilated?

He stumbles on like a rumor of war, huge
Threatening. Neighbors use the subterfuge

Of curtains. He stumbles down our short street
Thankfully passing us. I pause, wait,

Then to breathe relief lean on the sill
And for a second only my blood is still

With atavism. That rose he smashed frays
Ribboned across our hedge, recalling days

Of burned countryside, illicit braid:
A cause ruined before, a world betrayed.

The Famine Road

"Idle as trout in light Colonel Jones
these Irish, give them no coins at all; their bones
need toil, their characters no less." Trevelyan's
seal blooded the deal table. The Relief
Committee deliberated: "Might it be safe,
Colonel, to give them roads, roads to force
from nowhere, going nowhere of course?"

one out of every ten and then
another third of those again
women—in a case like yours.

Sick, directionless they worked. Fork, stick
were iron years away; after all could
they not blood their knuckles on rock, suck
April hailstones for water and for food?
Why for that, cunning as housewives, each eyed—
as if at a corner butcher—the other's buttock.

anything may have caused it, spores,
a childhood accident; one sees
day after day these mysteries.

Dusk: they will work tomorrow without him.
They know it and walk clear. He has become
a typhoid pariah, his blood tainted, although
he shares it with some there. No more than snow
attends its own flakes where they settle
and melt, will they pray by his death rattle.

You never will, never you know
but take it well woman, grow
your garden, keep house, good-bye.

"It has gone better than we expected, Lord
Trevelyan, sedition, idleness, cured
in one. From parish to parish, field to field;
the wretches work till they are quite worn,
then fester by their work. We march the corn
to the ships in peace. This Tuesday I saw bones
out of my carriage window. Your servant Jones."

*Barren, never to know the load
of his child in you, what is your body
now if not a famine road?*

Child of Our Time

(FOR AENGUS)

Yesterday I knew no lullaby
But you have taught me overnight to order
This song, which takes from your final cry
Its tune, from your unreasoned end its reason;
Its rhythm from the discord of your murder
Its motive from the fact you cannot listen.

We who should have known how to instruct
With rhymes for your waking, rhythms for your sleep,
Names for the animals you took to bed,
Tales to distract, legends to protect
Later an idiom for you to keep
And living, learn, must learn from you dead,

To make our broken images rebuild
Themselves around your limbs, your broken
Image, find for your sake whose life our idle
Talk has cost, a new language. Child
Of our time, our times have robbed your cradle.
Sleep in a world your final sleep has woken.

17 May 1974
On a child killed in the Dublin bombing

The Hanging Judge

Come to the country where justice is seen to be done.
Done daily. Come to the country where
Sentence is passed by word of mouth and raw
Boys are killed for it. Look, here
We hanged our son. Our only son.
And hang him still. And still we call it law.

James Lynch Fitzstephen. Magistrate.
First Citizen of Galway. 1493.
Spanish merchant trader, his horror
Of deceit a byword. A pillar of society.
With one weakness, Walter, whose every trait
Reversed his like a signature in a mirror.

Torches splutter. The dancing, supple,
Spanish-taught, starts. James Lynch Fitzstephen
May disapprove but he, a man of principle,
Recalls young Gomez is a guest in town,
And the girl beside him, his son's choice, may restore
A new name and honor to his heir.

Dawn. Gomez dead, in a wood. The Spanish heart
Which softened to her rigid with the steel
Of Walter Lynch's blade. Wild justice there—
Now to its restraint, but not repeal,
He returns to Galway, friendless, to be met,
In the city, by his father. In the stare

Which passed slowly between them, a history
Pauses: repression and rebellion, the scaffold
And its songs, the principle unsung
Are clues in this narration to a mystery
Even now unsolved, and only to be told
As a ghost story against a haunting—

As you, father, haunt me. The rope trails
From your fingers. Below you the abyss.
Your arms balanced as the scales of justice,
You tie the blindfold. Then from your own eyes fall scales.
But too late. Tears of doubt. Tears of remorse.
Dropping on your own neck like a noose.

A Soldier's Son

A young man's war it is, a young man's war,
Or so they say and so they go to wage
This struggle where, armored only in nightmare,
Every warrior is under age—
A son seeing each night leave, as father,
A man who may become the ancestor

In a backstreet stabbing, at a ghetto corner
Of future wars and further fratricide.
Son of a soldier who saw war on the ground,
Now cross the peace lines I have made for you
To find on this side if not peace then honor,
Your heritage, knowing as I do

That in the cross-hairs of his gun he found
You his only son, and when he aimed
And when the bullet cracked, the only sound
Was of his son rifling his heart. You twist
That heart today. You are his killed, his maimed.
He is your war. You are his pacifist.

The Greek Experience

Until that night, the night I lost my wonder,
He was my deity. First of my mentors.
   Master craftsman he; mere apprentice
   I, hearing how Croesus, to entice
   The priestess predators
Wooed a false oracle. But mine the truth
I thought, marveling at Cyrus tuned to plunder
By oboes, playing on Persia. But who cares now?
My name means nothing here. His, Herodotus,

Towers in Babylon, salts the Aegean
Is silted into each Ionic ear.
   Only I know the charlatan
   The mountebank who tongued
   Day slyly to night
To suit his purpose. Prepared to be harangued
And angled by his anecdotes, his school
Of stories, instead I found that night
A mind incapable of insight as a mule

Of generation. "The times need iron men,
Pragmatists," he said, "who can devise
   For those problems which arise
   So frequently, a swift solution.
   A man such as this:
He is a soldier, able to lead, to train.
His stallion where the Gyndes finds the Tigris
And those two rivers join in dissolution
In the Gulf, drowned. The waters combed its mane.

"Now he was leading Persian against Mede
But called a truce, cut his troops in two
   And swore revenge upon the water.
   He was the first to take his blade,
   The first to teach the lesson

With stabs and thrusts. He prolonged the slaughter
All summer long. The river now is channeled.
Those are the men we need." I listened, chilled.
"A soldier is lost to us. Now a deadly assassin

"Lies in wait for us all," was my recourse.
"Nonsense," he said. But I was trying to live
   The ambush, the sudden fever,
   The assault of a single force—
   An instant, the divider
Of a man from his own mind, his mythic source,
His origin in animal and primitive,
Which changes centaur into horse and rider—
The sort of wound a man might imitate forever.

And seeing hacked limbs, I was their screams,
Their first spasm of terror. But I was his dreams
   Also as, victim to his victim,
   He saw himself split again
   And turned away alone,
Forever puzzled. "He will kill again of course,"
I said. He smiled and sneered. "I am
The traveler after all. You can't have known
How hard it is to get a good horse."

The Laws of Love

(FOR MARY ROBINSON)

At first light the legislator
Who schooled you, creator
Of each force, each element,
Its secret law, its small print
Nature—while dawn, baptismal as waters
which broke early in dark, began—
First saw the first of your daughters
Become in your arms a citizen.

How easy for you to have made
For her a perfumed stockade,
How easy for you to impose
Laws and structures, torts for those
Fragments which matter less and less
As all fragments, and we must bless
The child, its murderer, defend
This chaos somehow which must end

With order. But who can separate
Hatred from its opposite
Or judge which is the other's source
Today? Unless perhaps that force
Which makes your Moy in its ridge pool
Prime teenage trout for butchery,
While at the same time fulfill
The blood-tie of the tide, as we

Once new found sisters, each grown miser
With new found blood began to trade
Salmond for Shakespeare—none the wiser
Then but now I see it focus
Slowly—a miracle, a closing wound.
That sisters kill, that sisters die, must mock us
Now, unless, with separate speech we find
For them new blood, for them now plead

Another world for whose horizons,
For whose anguish no reprieve
Exists unless new citizens,
And, as we found, the laws of love—
We two whose very first words fell
Like wishes down a wishing well,
Ungranted, had we known, unwanted
Yet still there as the well is, haunted.

Sisters

(FOR NESSA MY OWN)

Now it is winter and the hare
Imitates the hillside snow,
Crouches in his frame of ice,
The dormouse in his wheel of fur,
While in caves hour by hour
The bat glistens in reverse.

Snowdrops poised for assassination
Broadcast, white in the face, the stress
Of first bursting out of a prison
Where winter grips the warder's keys
By day then, at the dusk's tilt,
Loops them to Orion's belt.

In Monkstown bay a young seal
Surfaces, sleuth hound of herring;
Gulls shriek as he steals their meal
But I, getting the hint of spring,
As a fisherman an Armada hull,
Welcome his unexpected skull

For you, as his outline through
The spring tide comes to view;
Spring to mind. In such disguise
Our love survived as the sea with ease
Becomes with granite a graphic twin
Tumbling like a harlequin.

At seven years, the age of reason,
The ready child communicates
With Christ, according to our church.
Seven years ago, in the silly season,
And for such reasons, our two hearts
Were put outside each other's reach.

The fable goes, becoming warmer
Every second against his breast:
Christ's blood created the first informer,
The robin redbreast. And still the thirst
For knowledge and blood, they still remain,
And still we turn to still the pain.

O and my sister, not a sound,
Could find its way into this silence,
Nor intervene where you have found
In one stunned heart, which must now trounce
Breaking, if not a breathing space,
Well then a sister's grim embrace.

And in your ear a final word—
That we remember all our pain
Has saved us from a final fate,
One worse than death. Has left us scarred
But strangely safe for we remain
From these others separate.

The three harridans who toy
With human life, who in the cut
And thrust of gossip, never
Noticed one untwisted joy,
One sisterhood and could not sever
Ours with a chill and idle gesture.

II

O Fons Bandusiae

(Horace 3:XIII)

Bold as crystal, bright as glass,
Your waters leap while we appear
Carrying to your woodland shrine
Gifts below your worthiness,
Grape and flower, Bandusia,
Yellow hawksbeard, ready wine.

And tomorrow we will bring
A struggling kid, his temples sore
With early horns, as sacrifice.
Tomorrow his new trumpeting
Will come to nothing, when his gore
Stains and thaws your bright ice.

Canicula, the lamp of drought,
The summer's fire, leaves your grace
Inviolate in the woods where
Everyday you spring to comfort
The broad bull in his trace,
The herd out of the shepherd's care.

With every fountain, every spring
Of legend, I will set you down
In praise and immortal spate:
These waters which drop gossiping
To ground, this wet surrounding stone
And this green oak I celebrate.

Chorus of the Shadows

(after Nelly Sachs)

Puppets we are, strung by a puppet master.
He knows the theater of the absurd. He understands
Murder too well. Outrage. Grief. Disaster.
He puts the show on in hell. By his permission
We are moths fired and turned on his obsession.
His hands,

Are pinned to the dust. They darken the hangman's threats,
Give depth to the noose and our dimensions greet him,
The victim, as he plummets. No wonder we are
Weary of our own silhouettes.
Now we are driven to it, now we deliver
An ultimatum

To the planet which scripts our part. Take away
Light and we will not undertake love
Any longer. Give us a new part to play
In the day of a child or a stake in the luck—the frail
Perfect luck—of a dragonfly above
The rim of a well.

From the Irish of Pangur Ban

(FOR MAIRIN)

Myself and Pangur, cat and sage
Go each about our business;
I harrass my beloved page,
He his mouse.

Fame comes second to the peace
Of study, a still day.
Unenvious, Pangur's choice
Is child's play.

Neither bored, both hone
At home a separate skill,
Moving, after hours alone,
To the kill.

And when at last his net wraps,
After a sly fight,
Around a mouse, mine traps
Sudden insight.

On my cell wall here,
His sight fixes. Burning.
Searching. My old eyes peer
At new learning.

His delight when his claws
Close on his prey
Equals mine, when sudden clues
Light my way.

So we find by degrees
Peace in solitude,
Both of us—solitaries—
Have each the trade

He loves. Pangur, never idle
Day or night
Hunts mice. I hunt each riddle
From dark to light.

The Atlantic Ocean

(after Mayakovsky)

This stone, this Spanish stone, flings light
Like acid in my eyes. Walls splice the day.
Our freighter chokes, then belches anthracite,
Fresh water up by noon. We are away.
   A shrivelled Europe faces
   Starboard. Our guzzling boat
   Bloats on fish, swallows, chases
   The anchor down its throat.

Waves are conjurors, splashes sleeves,
Up which aces of past and future hide.
One man finds love, another what he grieves
By watching. To me they are another side
   Of life, not one to do
   With retrospect or manners
   But with the ballyhoo
   Of war, the hoist of banners.

Out of this ocean now, its menacing storms,
Out of its cryptic structures, its tribal
Tides, out of its secret order, from the cabal
Of trade wind and water, look, a Soviet forms!
   A squad of drops batters
   The sky for a second, wears
   Out its force, then turns and tears
   Each imperial crest to tatters.

The waves are agitating now, the sea
Itself becomes the theater of the battle.
Lesser waves congregate, they settle
On a policy for all. All agree
   Not to abandon their will
   To fight, their fierce airs
   Their stormy posture until
   Victory is theirs.

So what has started well can flourish still,
As for example, underneath the tide
The marvel of structured self-perfecting coral—
Now a milestone, soon to be a guide
    To the she-whale, the sperm-whale nosing
    Clear of the shark, the porpoises
    Braceleting the ships' bows.
    The octopus intricately dozing.

No wonder it beats like an alternate heart in me,
No wonder its drops fill and fall from my eyes
In familiar drops. It's in the family.
At last I see, at last I recognize
    In its wild station,
    Its ice and riot, its other
    Prowess, of my revolution
    The elder brother.

Conversation with an Inspector of Taxes about Poetry

(after Mayakovsky)

No, Comrade Inspector, I won't sit down.
Thank you. Forgive me taking your time.
What a delicate matter this business of mine
Is! The more difficult since I am
Concerned to discern the role of the poet
Within the ranks of the proletariat.

If you knew how you've added to my troubles
Taxing me like a shopkeeper or kulak!
For six months you claim five hundred rubles.
And twenty-five for the forms I didn't send back.
But I work as hard as the rest. Look what I've lost
In production. See what my materials cost.

Perhaps I should explain it in your idiom.
What you would call a promissory note
Is roughly the equivalent of a rhyme
To us, owed to each and every alternate
Line. And then in the petty cash of sense
We moisten the coins of nuance.

Suppose I select a word to go
Into a line. It doesn't fit. I start
To force it. The next thing I know
The seams of the stanza strain apart.
Comrade Inspector, I can give
Assurances that words are expensive.

I revert now to poetic license:
Metaphorically speaking my rhyming
Is a keg of dynamite, my lines
Smolder towards it. Then the timing
Device detonates and finally
The whole poem blows sky high.

Accusing me from your questionnaire
I see *Have you traveled in the course
Of business*? But what if every year
I've bitted and stampeded Pegasus
Till both of us were worn? Have sense.
Take into account the following instance.

There may be in Venezuela five
Or six sweet rhymes undiscovered.
If in pursuit of them I have
Tax to pay on travel, then my fevered
Search would draw too mean a loan
For poetry to sack the unknown.

Considering all this will you allow
Me a small mercenary reprieve?
I'll accept an inch of clay, a plow.
I'll be a peasant. Otherwise I achieve
So little by this speech that its effect,
Nil on you, on me I expect,

Will be years from now, I am sure,
These lines like ones in a puppet show,
Will jerk you back, inking your signature
On final demands. So, Comrade, so
I will have guaranteed your encore
Years after I have died and lie a pauper—

Crushed not by you bureaucrat
Though your claims are irritating, true,
But by the vast claims on a poet
I could not meet. All my debts to you
Are those of any chance financial sinner
But these to follow are my debts of honor:

To the Red Army, boiling across frontiers
In a wash of Cossack stallions, coats
Threaded from goat hide, unshaved hairs
Masking them like bandits, their supporters
Cheering them as the musket shots
Ventilated each of their deserters.

To the winter flowering cherry of Japan,
Frail as a foundling which never found
In my verse even the shelter given
To it by the snows which surround
Its blossom stealthily as rags are heaped
Over a sprawled vagrant while he sleeps.

Finally I know myself indebted,
Beyond anything I can return,
To the fastness of my winter cradle.
Because somehow I never celebrated
Its bleak skies. To this day they remain
Unsung and my tongue is idle.

III

Ode to Suburbia

Six o'clock: the kitchen bulbs which blister
Your dark, your housewives starting to nose
Out each other's day, the claustrophobia
Of your back gardens varicose
With shrubs, make an ugly sister
Of you suburbia.

How long ago did the glass in your windows subtly
Silver into mirrors which again
And again show the same woman
Shriek at a child? Which multiply
A dish, a brush, ash,
The gape of a fish.

In the kitchen, the gape of a child in the cot?
You swelled so that when you tried
The silver slipper on your foot
It pinched your instep and the common
Hurt which touched you made
You human.

No creature of the streets will feel the touch
Of a wand turning the wet sinews
Of fruit suddenly to a coach,
While this rat without leather reins
Or a whip or britches continues
Sliming your drains.

No magic here. Yet you encroach until
The shy countryside, fooled
By your plainness, falls, then rises
From your bed changed, schooled
Forever by your skill,
Your compromises.

Midnight and your metamorphosis
Is now complete, although the mind
Which spinstered you might still miss
Your mystery now, might still fail
To see your power defined
By this detail.

By this creature drowsing now in every house—
The same lion who tore stripes
Once off zebras. Who now sleeps,
Small beside the coals. And may
On a red letter day
Catch a mouse.

Naoise at Four

The trap baited for them snaps.
like forest pests they fall for it,
like humans writhe, like both submit.
Three brothers die: their three saps
spill until their split kith
heals into an Irish myth

Naoise, named for one of these,
you stand in our kitchen, sip
milk from a plastic cup
from our cupboard. Our unease
vanishes with one smile
as each suburban, modern detail

distances us from old lives.
Yet every night on our screens
new ones are lost. Wounds open.
Nothing heals. And what perspective
on this sudden Irish fury
can solve it to a folk memory?

Cyclist with Cut Branches

Country hands on the handlebars,
A bicycle bisecting cars
   Lethal and casual
In rush hour traffic, I remember
Seeing, as I watched that September
   For you as usual.

Like rapid mercury abused
By summer heat where it is housed
   In slender telling glass
My heart taking grief's temperature
That summer, lost its powers to cure,
   Its gift to analyze.

Jasmine and the hyacinth,
The lintel mortar and the plinth
   Of spring across his bars,
Like globed grapes at first I thought
Then at last more surely wrought
   Like winter's single stars.

Until I glimpsed not him but you
Like an animal the packs pursue
   To covert in a forest,
And knew the branches were not spring's
Nor even summer's ample things,
   But decay's simple trust.

And since we had been like them cut
But from the flowering not the root
   Then we had thanks to give—
That they and we had opened once,
Had found the light, had lost its glance
   And still had lives to live.

Song

Where in blind files
Bats outsleep the frost
Too fast, too fast
For ice, afraid he'd slip
By me I asked him first.

Round as a bracelet
Clasping the wet grass,
An adder drowsed by berries
Which change blood to cess.
Dreading delay's venom
I risked the first kiss.

My skirt in my hand.
Lifting my hem high
I forded the river there.
Drops splashed my thigh.
Ahead of me at last
He turned at my cry:

"Look how the water comes
Boldly to my side.
See the waves attempt
What you have never tried."
And he late that night
Followed the leaping tide.

The Botanic Gardens

(FOR KEVIN)

Guided by love, leaving aside dispute—
Guns on the pages of newspapers, the sound
Urgent of peace—we drive in real pursuit
Of another season, spring, where each has found
Something before, new, and then sense
In the Botanic Gardens, terms of reference.

You take my hand. Three years ago, your bride,
I felt your heart in darkness, a full moon
Hauling mine to it like a tide.
Still at night our selves reach to join.
To twine like these trees in peace and stress
Before the peril of unconsciousness.

Corsican pine, guerrilla poison plants,
The first gardener here by foreign carriage
And careful seeding in this circumference
Imitated the hours of our marriage:
The flowers of forced proximity, swollen, fed,
Flourishing here, usually sheltered,

Exposed this once.
                              Now you have overstepped
My reach, searching for something this February
Like a scholar in poor light over a script,
Able at last to decipher its coded story.
And so preoccupied you do not see
My absence in the conservatory

Where you, while African grotesqueries
Sweat in sandy heat, at last stand
Wondering at cacti, deformed trees
Most ridicule. Each pumpkin history
Turns coach at a touch of your hand.

I watch and love you in your mystery.

Prisoners

I saw him first lost in the lion cages
of the zoo. Before he could tear it out,
I screamed my heart out. But his rages
had been left behind. All he had left was his lope,
his mane as—bored as a socialite
with her morning post—I saw him slit
A rabbit open like an envelope.

Everything after that was parody:

I glimpsed him at the hearth in a jet
cat, in a school annual tamed in type,
in a screen safari. The irony
of finding him here in the one habitat
I never expected—alive and well in our suburban

world, present as I garden, sweep,
wring the teacloth dry, domesticate
acanthus in a bowl, orbit each chair
exactly round our table. Your pullover
lies on the bed upstairs, spread out where
you can no more free yourself from the bars
of your arms round me than can over us

the lion flee, silently, his stars.

Ready for Flight

From this I will not swerve nor fall nor falter:
If around your heart the crowds disperse,
And I who at their whim now freeze or swelter
Am allowed to come to a more temperate place.
And if a runner starts to run to me
Dispatched by you, crying that all is trampled
Underfoot, terraces smashed, the entry
Into holy places rudely sampled,

Then I would come at once my love with love
Bringing to wasted areas the sight

Of butterfly and swan and turtle dove
Their wings ruffled like sails ready for flight.

In such surroundings, after the decease
Of devils, you and I would live in peace.

Anon

I sympathize but wonder what he fled
From: the press, an unimpressed boss,
His wife smirking as he came to bed,
Aunts whispering that he'd turned to verse
As though to vice?
   Maybe they weren't far wrong.
Some guilty midnight, the idea spawned, shawled
In words, he abandoned it, a foundling
To be forever afterwards the love child
Of anthologies. Then back to work,
His moment's indiscretion a secret
Until one day rifling through a book
To find it, accusing, illegitimate.

Suburban Woman

I

Town and country at each other's throat—
between a space of truce until one night

walls began to multiply, to spawn
like lewd whispers of the goings-on,

the romperings, the rape on either side.
The smiling killing. That you were better dead

than let them get you. But they came, armed
with blades and ladders, with slimed

knives, day after day, week by week—
a proxy violation. She woke

one morning to the usual story. Withdrawing
neither side had gained, but there, dying,

caught in cross fire, her past lay. Like a pride
of lions toiled for booty, tribal acres died

and her world with them. She saw their power to sever
with a scar. She is the sole survivor.

II

Morning, mistress of talcums, spun
and second cottons, run tights
she is, courtesan to the lethal
rapine of routine. The room invites.

She reaches to fluoresce the dawn.
The kitchen lights like a brothel.

III

The chairs dusted and the morning
coffee break behind, she starts pawning

her day again to the curtains, the red
carpets, the stair rods, at last to the bed

the unmade bed where once in an underworld
of limbs, his eyes freckling the night like jeweled

lights on a cave wall, she, crying, stilled
bargained out of nothingness her child,

bartered from the dark her only daughter.
Waking, her cheeks dried, to a brighter

dawn she sensed in her as in April earth
a seed, a life ransoming her death.

IV

Late, quiet across her garden
sunlight shifts like a cat
burglar, thieving perspectives,
leaving her in the last light
alone, where, as shadows harden,
lengthen, silent she perceives
veteran dead-nettles, knapweed
crutched on walls, a summer's seed
of roses trenched in peat moss, and stares
at her life falling with her flowers,
like military tribute, or the tears
of shell-shocked men, into arrears.

V

Her kitchen blind down—a white flag—
the day's assault over, now she will shrug

a hundred small surrenders off as images
stillborn, unwritten metaphors, blank pages.

And on this territory, blindfold, we meet
at last, veterans of a defeat

no truce will heal, no formula prevent
breaking out fresh again. Again the print

of twigs stalking her pillow will begin
a new day and all her victims then—

hopes unreprieved, hours taken hostage—
will newly wake, while I, on a new page

will watch, like town and country, word, thought
look for ascendancy, poise, retreat

leaving each line maimed, my forces used.
Defeated we survive, we two, housed

together in my compromise, my craft—
who are of one another the first draft.

from

In Her Own Image
1980

Tirade for the Mimic Muse

I've caught you out. You slut. You fat trout
So here you are fumed in candle-stink.
Its yellow balm exhumes you for the glass.
How you arch and pout in it!
How you poach your face in it!
Anyone would think you were a whore—
An aging out-of-work kind-hearted tart.
I know you for the ruthless bitch you are:
Our criminal, our tricoteuse, our Muse—
Our Muse of Mimic Art.

Eye shadow, swivel brushes, blushers,
Hot pinks, rouge pots, sticks,
Ice for the pores, a mud mask—
All the latest tricks.
Not one of them disguise
That there's a dead millennium in your eyes.
You try to lamp the sockets of your loss:
The lives that famished for your look of love.
Your time is up. There's not a stroke, a flick
Can make your crime cosmetic.

With what drums and dances, what deceits
Rituals and flatteries of war,
Chants and pipes and witless empty rites
And war-like men
And wet-eyed patient women
You did protect yourself from horrors,
From the lizarding of eyelids
From the whiskering of nipples,
From the slow betrayals of our bedroom mirrors—
How you fled

The kitchen screw and the rack of labor,
The wash thumbed and the dish cracked,

The scream of beaten women,
The crime of babies battered,
The hubbub and the shriek of daily grief
That seeks asylum behind suburb walls—
A world you could have sheltered in your skirts—
And well I know and how I see it now,
The way you latched your belt and twitched your hem
And shook it off like dirt.

And I who mazed my way to womanhood
Through all your halls of mirrors, making faces,
To think I waited on your trashy whim!
Hoping your lamp and flash,
Your glass, might show
This world I needed nothing else to know
But love and again love and again love.
In a nappy stink, by a soaking wash
Among stacked dishes
Your glass cracked,

Your luck ran out. Look. My words leap
Among your pinks, your stench pots and sticks.
They scatter shadow, swivel brushes, blushers.
Make your face naked,
Strip your mind naked,
Drench your skin in a woman's tears.
I will wake you from your sluttish sleep.
I will show you true reflections, terrors.
You are the Muse of all our mirrors.
Look in them and weep.

In Her Own Image

It is her eyes:
the irises are gold
and round they go
like the ring on my wedding finger,
round and round

and I can't touch
their histories or tears.
To think they were once my satellites!
They shut me out now.
Such light-years!

She is not myself
anymore she is not
even in my sky
anymore and I
am not myself.

I will not disfigure
her pretty face.
Let her wear amethyst thumbprints,
a family heirloom,
a sort of burial necklace

and I know just the place:
Where the wall glooms,
where the lettuce seeds,
where the jasmine springs
no surprises

I will bed her.
She will bloom there,
second nature to me,
the one perfection
among compromises.

In His Own Image

I was not myself, myself.
The celery feathers,
the bacon flitch,
the cups deep on the shelf
and my cheek
coppered and shone
in the kettle's paunch,
my mouth
blubbed in the tin of the pan—
they were all I had to go on.

How could I go on
With such meager proofs of myself?
I woke day after day.
Day after day I was gone.
From the self I was last night.

And then he came home tight.

Such a simple definition!
How did I miss it?
Now I see
that all I needed
was a hand
to mold my mouth
to scald my cheek,
was this concussion
by whose lights I find
my self-possession,
where I grow complete.

He splits my lip with his fist,
shadows my eye with a blow,
knuckles my neck to its proper angle.
What a perfectionist!

His are a sculptor's hands:
they summon
form from the void,
they bring
me to myself again.
I am a new woman.

Anorexic

Flesh is heretic.
My body is a witch.
I am burning it.

Yes I am torching
her curves and paps and wiles.
They scorch in my self-denials.

How she meshed my head
in the half-truths
of her fevers till I renounced
milk and honey
and the taste of lunch.

I vomited
her hungers.
Now the bitch is burning.

I am starved and curveless.
I am skin and bone.
She has learned her lesson.

Thin as a rib
I turn in sleep.
My dreams probe

a claustrophobia
a sensuous enclosure.
How warm it was and wide

once by a warm drum,
once by the song of his breath
and in his sleeping side.

Only a little more,
only a few more days
sinless, foodless.

I will slip
back into him again
as if I have never been away.

Caged so
I will grow
angular and holy

past pain
keeping his heart
such company

as will make me forget
in a small space
the fall

into forked dark,
into python needs
heaving to hips and breasts
and lips and heat
and sweat and fat and greed.

Mastectomy

My ears heard
their words.
I didn't believe them.

No, even through my tears
they couldn't deceive me.
Even so

I could see
through them
to the years

opening
their arteries,
fields gulching

into trenches
cuirasses stenching,
a mulch of heads

and towns
as prone
to bladed men

as women.
How well
I recognized

the specialist
freshing death
across his desk,

the surgeon,
blade-handed,
standing there

urging patience.
How well
they have succeeded!

I have stopped bleeding
I look down.
It has gone.
So they have taken off
what slaked them first,
what they have hated since:

blue-veined
white-domed
home

of wonder
and the wetness
of their dreams.

I flatten
to their looting,
to the sleight

of their plunder.
I am a brute site.
Theirs is the true booty.

Solitary

Night:
An oratory of dark,
a chapel of unreason.

Here in the shrubbery
the shrine.
I am its votary,
its season.

Flames
single
to my fingers

expert
to pick out
their heart,
the sacred heat

none may violate.
You could die for this.
The gods could make you blind.

I defy them.
I know,
only I know

these incendiary
and frenzied ways:
I am alone.

No one's here,
no one sees
my hands

fan and cup,
my thumbs tinder.
How it leaps

from spark to blaze!
I flush
I darken.

How my flesh summers,
how my mind shadows
meshed in this brightness.

How my cry
blasphemes
light and dark,
screams
land from sea,
makes word flesh
that now makes me

animal
inanimate, satiate,

and back I go
to a slack tip,
a light.

I stint my worship,
the cold watch I keep.
Fires flint somewhere else.
I winter
into sleep.

Menses

It is dark again.

I am sick of it
filled with it,
dulled by it,
thick with it.

To be the mere pollution of her wake!
a water cauled by her light,
a slick haul,
a fallen self,
a violence,
a daughter.

I am the moon's looking-glass.
My days are moon-dials.
She will never be done with me.
She needs me.
She is dry.

I leash to her,
a sea,
a washy heave,
a tide.
Only my mind is free

among the ruffian growths,
the bindweed
and the meadowsweet,
the riff-raff of my garden.

How I envy them;
each filament,
each anther bred
from its own style,

its stamen,
is to itself a christening,
is to itself a marriage bed.

They fall to earth,
so ignorant
so innocent
of the sweated waters
and the watered salts,
of ecstasy,
of birth.

They are street-walkers,
lesbians,
nuns.
I am not one of them

and how they'd pity me

now as dusk encroaches
and she comes
looking for her looking-glass.
And it is me.

Yes it is me
she poaches her old face in.
I am bloated with her waters.
I am barren with her blood.
Another hour
and she will addle me

till I begin
to think like her.
As when I've grown
round and obscene with child,
or when I moan,
for him between the sheets,
then I begin to know
that I am bright and original
and that my light's my own.

Witching

My gifts
are nightly,
shifty, bookish.

By my craft
I bald the grass,
abort the birth

of calves
and warts.
I study dark.

Another age
and I'd have been
waisted

in a hedgy rage
of prejudice
and hate.

But times have changed.
They will be brought
to book.

these my enemies—
and bell
and candle too—

who breed
and breed,
who talk and talk—

birth
and bleeding,
the bacteria of feeds.

Midnight.
Now I own
the earth

The witching hour.
You'd think
you'd think

the bitches
couldn't reach
me here.

But here they are.
The nursery lights
they shine, they shine,

they multiply
they douse
mine!

But I
know
what to do:

I will
reverse
their arson,

make
a pyre of my haunch

and so
the last thing
they know

will be
the stench
of my crotch.

Flaming
tindering
I'll single

a page
of history
for these my sisters

for those kin
they kindled.
Yes it's my turn

to stack
the twigs
and twig the fire

and smell
how well

a woman's
flesh
can burn.

Exhibitionist

I wake to dark,
a window slime of dew.
Time to start

working
from the text,
making

from this trash
and gimmickry
of sex
my aesthetic:

a hip first,
a breast,
a slow
shadow strip
out of clothes

that busheled me
asleep.
What an artist am I!

Barely light
and yet—
cold shouldering

clipped laurel,
nippling the road—
I subvert

sculpture,
the old mode;
I skin

I dimple clay,
I flesh,
I rump stone.

This is my way—
to strip and strip
until

my dusk flush,
nude shade,
hush

of hip,
backbone,
thigh

blacks light
and I
become the night.

What stars
I harvest
to my dark!

Cast down
Lucifers,
spruce

businessmen,
their eyes
cast down.

I have them now.
I'll teach them now.
I'll show them how

in offices,
their minds
blind on files,

the view
blues through
my curves and arcs.

They are
a part
of my dark plan:

Into the gutter
of their lusts
I burn

the shine
of my flesh.
Let them know

for a change
the hate
and discipline,

the lusts
that prison
and the light that is

unyielding,
frigid,
constellate.

Making Up

My naked face;
I wake to it.
How it's dulsed and shrouded!
It's a cloud,

a dull pre-dawn.
But I'll soon
see to that.
I push the blusher up,

I raddle
and I prink,
pinking bone
till my eyes

are
a rouge-washed
flush on water.
Now the base

pales and wastes.
Light thins
from ear to chin,
whitening in

the ocean shine
mirror set
of my eyes
that I fledge

in old darks.
I grease and full
my mouth.
It won't stay shut:

I look
in the glass.
My face is made,
it says:

Take nothing, nothing
at its face value:
Legendary seas,
nakedness,

that up and stuck
lassitude
of thigh and buttock
that they prayed to—

it's a trick.
Myths
are made by men.
The truth of this

wave-raiding
sea-heaving
made-up
tale

of a face
from the source
of the morning
is my own:

Mine are the rouge pots,
the hot pinks,
the fledged
and edgy mix
of light and water
out of which
I dawn.

from
Night Feed
1982

Degas's Laundresses

You rise, you dawn
roll-sleeved Aphrodites,
out of a camisole brine,
a linen pit of stitches,
silking the fitted sheets
away from you like waves.

You seam dreams in the folds
of wash from which freshes
the whiff and reach of fields
where it bleached and stiffened.
Your chat's sabbatical:
brides, wedding outfits,

a pleasure of leisured women
are sweated into the folds,
the neat heaps of linen.
Now the drag of the clasp.
Your wrists basket your waist.
You round to the square weight.

Wait. There behind you.
A man. There behind you.
Whatever you do don't turn.
Why is he watching you?
Whatever you do don't turn.
Whatever you do don't turn.

See he takes his ease
staking his easel so,
slowly sharpening charcoal,
closing his eyes just so,
slowly smiling as if
so slowly he is

unbandaging his mind.
Surely a good laundress
would understand its twists,
its white turns,
its blind designs—

it's your winding sheet.

Woman in Kitchen

Breakfast over, islanded by noise,
she watches the machines go fast and slow.
She stands among them as they shake the house.
They move. Their destination is specific.
She has nowhere definite to go:
she might be a pedestrian in traffic.

White surfaces retract. White
sideboards light the white of walls.
Cups wink white in their saucers.
The light of day bleaches as it falls
on cups and sideboards. She could use
the room to tap with if she lost her sight.

Machines jigsaw everything she knows.
And she is everywhere among their furor:
the tropic of the dryer tumbling clothes.
The round lunar window of the washer.
The kettle in the toaster is a kingfisher
swooping for trout above the river's mirror.

The wash done, the kettle boiled, the sheets
spun and clean, the dryer stops dead.
The silence is a death. It starts to bury
the room in white spaces. She turns to spread
a cloth on the board and irons sheets
in a room white and quiet as a mortuary.

A Ballad of Beauty and Time

Plainly came the time
the eucalyptus tree
could not succor me,
nor the honey pot,
the sunshine vitamin.
Not even getting thin.
I had passed my prime.

Then, when bagged ash,
scalded quarts of water,
oil of the lime,
cinders for the skin
and honey all had failed,
I sorted out my money
and went to buy some time.

I knew the right address:
the occult house of shame
where all the women came
shopping for a mouth,
a new nose, an eyebrow
and entered without knocking
and stood as I did now.

A shape with a knife
stooped away from me
cutting something vague—
I couldn't really see—
it might have been a face.
I coughed once and said
—I want a lease of life.

The room was full of masks.
Lines of grins gaping.
A wall of skin stretching.

A chin he had re-worked,
a face he had re-made.
He slit and tucked and cut.
Then straightened from his blade.

"A tuck, a hem," he said—
"I only seam the line,
I only mend the dress.
It wouldn't do for you:
your quarrel's with the weave.
The best I achieve
is just a stitch in time."

I started out again.
I knew a studio
strewn with cold heels,
closed in marble shock.
I saw the sculptor there
chiseling a nose,
and buttonholed his smock:

"It's all very well
when you have bronzed a woman—
pinioned her and finned
wings on either shoulder.
Anyone can see
she won't get any older.
What good is that to me?

"See the last of youth
slumming in my skin,
my sham pink mouth.
Here behold your critic—
the threat to your aesthetic.
I am the brute proof.
Beauty is not truth."

"Truth is in our lies—"
he angrily replied.
"This woman fledged in stone,
the center of all eyes,
her own museum blind:

we sharpen with our skills
the arts of compromise.

"And all I have cast
in crystal or in glass,
in lapis or in onyx,
comes from my knowledge when—
above the honest flaw—
to lift and stay my hand
and say 'let it stand'."

It's a Woman's World

Our way of life
has hardly changed
since a wheel first
whetted a knife.

Maybe flame
burns more greedily,
and wheels are steadier
but we're the same

who milestone
our lives
with oversights—
living by the lights

of the loaf left
by the cash register,
the washing powder
paid for and wrapped,

the wash left wet:
like most historic peoples
we are defined
by what we forget,

by what we never will be—
star-gazers,
fire-eaters.
It's our alibi

for all time:
as far as history goes
we were never
on the scene of the crime.

So when the king's head
gored its basket—
grim harvest—
we were gristing bread

or getting the recipe
for a good soup
to appetize
our gossip.

It's still the same.
By night our windows
moth our children
to the flame

of hearth not history.
And still no page
scores the low music
of our outrage.

Appearances
still reassure:
that woman there,
craned to the starry mystery

is merely getting a breath
of evening air,
while this one here—
her mouth

a burning plume—
she's no fire-eater,
just my frosty neighbor
coming home.

Daphne with Her Thighs in Bark

I have written this

so that,
in the next myth,
my sister will be wiser.

Let her learn from me:

the opposite of passion
is not virtue
but routine.

Look at me.

I can be cooking,
making coffee,
scrubbing wood, perhaps,
and back it comes:
the crystalline, the otherwhere,
the wood

where I was
when he began the chase.
And how I ran from him!

Pan-thighed,
satyr-faced he was.

The trees reached out to me.
I silvered and
I quivered. I shook out
my foil of quick leaves.

He snouted past.
What a fool I was!

I shall be here forever,
setting out the tea,
among the coppers and the branching alloys and
the tin shine of this kitchen;
laying saucers on the pine table.

Save face, sister.
Fall. Stumble.
Rut with him.
His rough heat will keep you warm and

you will be better off than me,
with your memories
down the garden,
at the start of March,

unable to keep your eyes
off the chestnut tree—

just the way
it thrusts and hardens.

The New Pastoral

The first man had flint to spark. He had a wheel
to read his world.

I'm in the dark.

I am a lost, last inhabitant—
displaced person
in a pastoral chaos.

All day I listen to
the loud distress, the switch and tick of
new herds.

But I'm no shepherdess.

Can I unbruise these sprouts or cleanse this mud flesh
till it roots again?
Can I make whole
this lamb's knuckle, butchered from its last crooked suckling?

I could be happy here,
I could be something more than a refugee

were it not for this lamb unsuckled, for the nonstop
switch and tick
telling me

there was a past,
there was a pastoral,
and these chance sights

are little more than
amnesias of a rite

I danced once on a frieze.

The Woman Turns Herself into a Fish

Unpod
the bag,
the seed.

Slap
the flanks back.
Flatten

paps.
Make finny
scaled

and chill
the slack
and dimple

of the rump.
Pout
the mouth,

brow the eyes
and now
and now

eclipse
in these hips,
these loins

the moon,
the blood
flux.

It's done.
I turn,
I flab upward

blub-lipped,
hipless
and I am

sexless,
shed
of ecstasy,

a pale
swimmer,
sequin-skinned,

pearling eggs
screamlessly
in seaweed.

It's what
I set my heart on.
Yet

ruddering
and muscling
in the sunless tons

of new freedoms,
still
I feel

a chill pull,
a brightening,
a light, a light,

and how
in my loomy cold,
my greens,

still
she moons
in me.

The Woman Changes Her Skin

How often
in this loneliness,
unlighted
but for the porcelain

brightening
of the bath,
have I done this.
Again and again this.

This is the end:
This crepy
ruche of skin
papering my neck—

elastic when I smile!—
and my eyes
a purse of shadows—
it's time for something drastic to be done.

This time
in the shadowy
and woody light
between the bath and blind,

between the day and night,
the same blue
eye shadow,
rouge and blusher

will mesh
with my fingers
to a weavy
pulse.

In a ringed
coiling,
a convulsion
I will heave

to a sinuous
and final
shining off
of skin:

Look at the hood
I have made
for my eyes,
my head.

And how, quickly,
over my lips
slicked and cold
my tongue flickers.

Pose

(After the painting *Mrs. Badham* by Ingres)

She is a housekeeping. A spring cleaning.
A swept, tidied, emptied, kept woman.

Her rimmed hat, its unkempt streamers
neaten to the seams of a collar
frilled and pat as a dressing-table,
its pressed lace and ruching hardly able
to hide the solid column of her neck:
reckless fashion masking common sense!

She smirks uneasily at what she's shirking—
sitting on this chair in silly clothes,
posing in a truancy of frills.

There's no repose in her broad knees.
The shawl she shoulders just upholsters her.

She holds the open book like pantry keys.

Patchwork

I have been thinking at random
on the universe
or rather, how nothing in the universe
is random—

(there's nothing like presumption late at night.)

My sumptuous
trash bag of colors—
Laura Ashley cottons—
waits to be cut
and stitched and patched

but there's a mechanical feel
about the handle
of my secondhand sewing machine,
with its flowers
and *Singer* painted orange on it.
And its iron wheel.

My back is to the dark.
Somewhere out there
are stars and bits of stars
and little bits of bits.
And swiftness and brightness and drift.

But is it craft or art?

I will be here
till midnight,
cross-legged in the dining-room,
logging triangles and diamonds,
cutting and aligning,
finding greens in pinks

and burgundies in whites
until I finish it.

There's no reason in it.

Only when it's laid
right across the floor,
sphere on square
and seam on seam,
in a good light—
a night-sky spread—
will it start to hit me.

These are not bits.
They are pieces.

And the pieces fit.

Lights

We sailed the long way home
on a coal-burning ship.
There were bracelets on our freighter
of porpoises and water.

When we came where icebergs
mark the stars of The Bear
I leaned over the stern.
I was an urban twelve.

This was the Arctic garden.
A hard, sharkless Eden
porched by the North.
A snow-shrubbed orchard

with Aurora Borealis—
apple-green and icy—
behind an ice wall.
But I was a child of The Fall:

I loved the python waves—
their sinuous, tailing blaze—
coiled in polar water
shoaling towards the cold

occasions where the daughters
of myth sang for sailors,
who lay with them and lie
now in phosphor graves.

I lie half-awake.
The last star is out
and my book is shut.
These August dawns

green the sky at four.
The child asleep beside me
stirs away in dreams.
I am three times twelve.

No more the Aurora,
its apple-icy brightness.
But if I raise the window
and lean I can see

now over the garden,
its ice-cap of shadow,
a nursery light rising,
a midnight sun dawning.

The day will be the same—
its cold illusory rays,
the afternoon's enclosure
the dusk's ambiguous gleams:

Doubt still sharks
the close suburban night.
And all the lights I love
leave me in the dark.

Domestic Interior

1. Night Feed

This is dawn.
Believe me
This is your season, little daughter.
The moment daisies open,
The hour mercurial rainwater
Makes a mirror for sparrows.
It's time we drowned our sorrows.

I tiptoe in.
I lift you up
Wriggling
In your rosy, zipped sleeper.
Yes, this is the hour
For the early bird and me
When finder is keeper.

I crook the bottle.
How you suckle!
This is the best I can be,
Housewife
To this nursery
Where you hold on,
Dear life.

A silt of milk.
The last suck.
And now your eyes are open,
Birth-colored and offended.
Earth wakes.
You go back to sleep.
The feed is ended.

Worms turn.
Stars go in.
Even the moon is losing face.
Poplars stilt for dawn
And we begin
The long fall from grace.
I tuck you in.

2. Monotony

The stilled hub
and polar drab
of the suburb
closes in.

In the round
of the staircase,
my arms sheafing nappies,
I grow in and down

to an old spiral,
a well of questions,
an oracle:
will it tell me—

am I
at these altars,
warm shrines,
washing machines, dryers

with their incense
of men and infants
priestess
or sacrifice?

My late tasks
wait like children:
milk bottles,
the milkman's note.

Cold air
clouds the rinsed,

milky glass,
blowing clear

with a hint
of winter constellations:
will I find
my answer where

Virgo reaps?
Her arms sheafing
the hemisphere,
hour after frigid hour,

her virgin stars,
her maidenhead
married to force,
harry us

to wed our gleams
to brute routines:
solstices,
small families.

3. Hymn

For a.m.
December.
A lamb
would perish out there.

The cutlery glitter
of that sky
has nothing in it
I want to follow.

Here is the star
of my nativity:
a nursery lamp
in a suburb window

behind which
is boiled glass, a bottle
and a baby all
hisses like a kettle.

The light goes out.
The blackbird takes up his part.

I wake by habit.
I know it all by heart:

these candles
and the altar
and the psaltery of dawn.

And in the dark
as we slept
the world
was made flesh.

4. Partings

By the mercy
of the nursery light,
on the nursery wall,

among bears,
rattles, rag dolls—
in their big shadows—

we are one more and
inseparable again.
Day begins.

The world lives down
the dark union
of its wonders.

Your fingers fist in mine.
Outside the window
winter earth

discovers its horizon
as I cradle mine—

and light finds us
with the other loves
dawn sunders
to define.

5. Energies

This is my time:
The twilight closing in,
a hissing on the ring,
stove noises, kettle steam
and children's kisses.

But the energy of flowers!
Their faces are so white—
my garden daisies—
they are so tight-fisted,
such economies of light.

In the dusk they have made hay:
in a banked radiance,
in an acreage of brightness
they are misering the day
while mine delays away

in chores left to do:
the soup, the bath, the fire
then bed-time,
up the stairs—
and there, there

the buttery curls,
the light,
the bran-fur of the teddy bear,
the fist like a night-time daisy,
damp and tight.

6. The Muse Mother

My window pearls wet.
The bare rowan tree
berries rain.

I can see
from where I stand
a woman hunkering—
her busy hand
worrying a child's face,

working a nappy liner
over his sticky, loud
round of a mouth.

Her hand's a cloud
across his face,
making light and rain,
smiles and a frown,
a smile again.

She jockeys him to her hip,
pockets the nappy liner,
collars rain on her nape
and moves away

but my mind stays fixed:

If I could only decline her—
lost noun
out of context,
stray figure of speech—
from this rainy street

again to her roots,
she might teach me
a new language:

to be a sibyl
able to sing the past
in pure syllables,
limning hymns sung
to belly wheat or a woman—

able to speak at last
my mother tongue.

7. Endings

A child
shifts in a cot.
No matter what happens now
I'll never fill one again.

It's a night
white things ember in:
jasmine and the shine—
flowering, opaline—
of the apple trees.

If I lean
I can see
what it is the branches end in:

The leaf.
The reach.
The blossom.
The abandon.

8. In the Garden

Let's go out now
before the morning
gets warm.
Get your bicycle,

your teddy bear—
the one that's penny-coloured
like your hair—
and come.

I want to show you
what
I don't exactly know.
We'll find out.

It's our turn
in this garden,
by this light,
among the snails

and daisies—
one so slow
and one so closed—
to learn.

I could show you things:
how the poplar root
is pushing through,
how your apple tree is doing,

how daisies
shut like traps.

But you're happy
as it is

and innocence
that until this
was just
an abstract water,

welling elsewhere
to refresh,
is risen here
my daughter:

before the dew,
before the bloom,
the snail was here.
The whole morning is his loom

and this is truth,
this is brute grace
as only instinct knows
how to live it:

turn to me
your little face.
It shows a trace still,
an inkling of it.

9. After a Childhood Away from Ireland

One summer
we slipped in at dawn
on plum-coloured water
in the sloppy quiet.

The engines
of the ship stopped.
There was an eerie
drawing near,

a noiseless coming head-on
of red roofs, walls,
dogs, barley stooks.
Then we were there.

Cobh.
Coming home.
I had heard of this:
the ground the emigrants

resistless, weeping,
laid their cheeks to,
put their lips to kiss.
Love is also memory.

I only stared.
What I had lost
was not land
but the habit of land:

whether of growing out of
or settling back on,

or being
defined by.

I climb
to your nursery.
I stand listening
to the dissonances

of the summer's day ending.
I bend to kiss you.
Your cheeks
are brick pink.

10. Fruit on a Straight-Sided Tray

When the painter takes the straight-sided tray
and arranges late melons with grapes and lemons,
the true subject is the space between them,

in which repose the pleasure of these ovals
is seen to be an assembly of possibilities;
a deliberate collection of cross purposes.

Gross blues and purples. Yellow and the shadow of bloom.
The room smells of metal polish. The afternoon sun
brings light but not heat and no distraction from

the study of absences, the science of relationships
on which the abstraction is made actual: such as
fruit on a straight-sided tray; a homely arrangement.

This is the geometry of the visible, physical tryst
between substances, disguising for a while the equation
that kills: you are my child and between us are

spaces. Distances. Growing to infinities.

11. Domestic Interior

The woman is as round
as the new ring
ambering her finger.
The mirror weds her.
She has long since been bedded.

There is
about it all
a quiet search for attention
like the unexpected shine
of a despised utensil.

The oils,
the varnishes,
the cracked light,
the worm of permanence—
all of them supplied by Van Eyck—

by whose edict she will stay
burnished, fertile,
on her wedding day,
interred in her joy.
Love, turn.

The convex of your eye
that is so loving, bright
and constant yet shows
only this woman in her varnishes,
who won't improve in the light.

But there's a way of life
that is its own witness:
put the kettle on, shut the blind.

Home is a sleeping child,
an open mind

and our effects,
shrugged and settled
in the sort of light
jugs and kettles
grow important by.

from
The Journey
1987

I Remember

I remember the way the big windows washed
out the room and the winter darks tinted
it and how, in the brute quiet and aftermath,
an eyebrow waited helplessly to be composed

from the palette with its scarabs of oil
colors gleaming through a dusk leaking from
the iron railings and the ruined evenings of
bombed-out, post-war London; how the easel was

mulberry wood and, porcupining in a jar,
the spines of my mother's portrait brushes
spiked from the dirty turpentine and the face
on the canvas was the scattered fractions

of the face which had come up the stairs
that morning and had taken up position in
the big drawing-room and had been still
and was now gone; and I remember, I remember

I was the interloper who knows both love and fear,
who comes near and draws back, who feels nothing
beyond the need to touch, to handle, to dismantle it,
the mystery; and how in the morning when I came down—

a nine-year-old in high, fawn socks—
the room had been shocked into a glacier
of cotton sheets thrown over the almond
and vanilla silk of the French Empire chairs.

Mise Eire

I won't go back to it—

my nation displaced
into old dactyls,
oaths made
by the animal tallows
of the candle—

land of the Gulf Stream,
the small farm,
the scalded memory,
the songs
that bandage up the history,
the words
that make a rhythm of the crime

where time is time past.
A palsy of regrets.
No. I won't go back.
My roots are brutal:

I am the woman—
a sloven's mix
of silk at the wrists,
a sort of dove-strut
in the precincts of the garrison—

who practices
the quick frictions,
the rictus of delight
and gets cambric for it,
rice-colored silks.

I am the woman
in the gansy-coat

on board the *Mary Belle*,
in the huddling cold,

holding her half-dead baby to her
as the wind shifts East
and North over the dirty
water of the wharf

mingling the immigrant
guttural with the vowels
of homesickness who neither
knows nor cares that

a new language
is a kind of scar
and heals after a while
into a passable imitation
of what went before.

Self-Portrait on a Summer Evening

Jean-Baptiste Chardin
is painting a woman
in the last summer light.

All summer long
he has been slighting her
in botched blues, tints,
half-tones, rinsed neutrals.

What you are watching
is light unlearning itself,
an infinite unfrocking of the prism.

Before your eyes
the ordinary life
is being glazed over:
pigments of the bibelot,
the cabochon, the water-opal
pearl to the intimate
simple colors of
her ankle-length summer skirt.

Truth makes shift:
The triptych shrinks
to the cabinet picture.

Can't you feel it?
Aren't you chilled by it?
The way the late afternoon
is reduced to detail—

the sky that odd shape of apron—

opaque, scumbled—
the lazulis of the horizon becoming

optical grays
before your eyes
before your eyes
in my ankle-length
summer skirt

crossing between
the garden and the house,
under the whitebeam trees,
keeping an eye on
the length of the grass,
the height of the hedge,
the distance of the children

I am Chardin's woman

edged in reflected light,
hardened by
the need to be ordinary.

The Oral Tradition

I was standing there
at the end of a reading
or a workshop or whatever,
watching people heading
out into the weather,

only half-wondering
what becomes of words,
the brisk herbs of language,
the fragrances we think we sing,
if anything.

We were left behind
in a firelit room
in which the color scheme
crouched well down—
golds, a sort of dun

a distressed ocher—
and the sole richness was
in the suggestion of a texture
like the low flax gleam
that comes off polished leather.

Two women
were standing in shadow,
one with her back turned.
Their talk was a gesture,
an outstretched hand.

They talked to each other
and words like "summer"
"birth" "great-grandmother"
kept pleading with me,
urging me to follow.

"She could feel it coming"—
one of them was saying—
"all the way there,
across the fields at evening
and no one there, God help her

"and she had on a skirt
of cross-woven linen
and the little one
kept pulling at it.
It was nearly night . . . "

(Wood hissed and split
in the open grate,
broke apart in sparks,
a windfall of light
in the room's darkness)

" . . . when she lay down
and gave birth to him
in an open meadow.
What a child that was
to be born without a blemish!"

It had started raining,
the windows dripping, misted.
One moment I was standing
not seeing out,
only half-listening

staring at the night; the next
- without warning
I was caught by it:
the bruised summer light,
the musical sub-text

of mauve eaves on lilac
and the laburnum past
and shadow where the lime
tree dropped its bracts
in frills of contrast

where she lay down
in vetch and linen
and lifted up her son
to the archive
they would shelter in:

the oral song
avid as superstition,
layered like an amber in
the wreck of language
and the remnants of a nation.

I was getting out
my coat, buttoning it,
shrugging up the collar.
It was bitter outside,
a real winter's night

and I had distances
ahead of me: iron miles
in trains, iron rails
repeating instances
and reasons; the wheels

singing innuendoes, hints,
outlines underneath
the surface, a sense
suddenly of truth,
its resonance.

Fever

is what remained or what they thought
remained after the ague and the sweats
were over and the shock of wild flowers
at the bedside had been taken away;

is what they tried to shake out of
the crush and dimple of cotton,
the shy dust of a bridal skirt;
is what they beat, lashed, hurt like

flesh as if it were a lack of virtue
in a young girl sobbing her heart out
in a small town for having been seen
kissing by the river; is what they burned

alive in their own back gardens
as if it were a witch and not the full-
length winter gaberdine and breathed again
when the fires went out in charred dew.

My grandmother died in a fever ward,
younger than I am and far from
the sweet chills of a Louth spring—
its sprigged light and its wild flowers—

with five orphan daughters to her name.
Names, shadows, visitations, hints
and a half-sense of half-lives remain.
And nothing else, nothing more unless

I re-construct the soaked-through midnights;
vigils; the histories I never learned
to predict the lyric of; and re-construct
risk; as if silence could become rage,

as if what we lost is a contagion
that breaks out in what cannot be
shaken out from words or beaten out
from meaning and survives to weaken

what is given, what is certain
and burns away everything but this
exact moment of delirium when
someone cries out someone's name.

The Unlived Life

"Listen to me," I said to my neighbor,
"how do you make a hexagon-shape template?"

So we talked about end papers,
cropped circles, block piece-work
while the children shouted and
the texture of synthetics as compared
with the touch of strong cloth
and how they both washed.

"You start out with jest so much caliker"—
Eliza Calvert Hall of Kentucky said—
"that's the predestination
but when it comes to cuttin' out
the quilt, why, you're free to choose."

Suddenly I could see us
calicoed, overawed, dressed in cotton
at the railroad crossing, watching
the flange-wheeled, steam-driven, iron omen
of another life passing, passing
wondering for a moment what it was
we were missing as we turned for home

to choose
in the shiver of silk and dimity
the unlived life, its symmetry
explored on a hoop with a crewel needle
under the silence of the oil light;

to formalize the terrors of routine
in the algebras of a marriage quilt
on alternate mornings when you knew
that all you owned was what you shared.

It was bed-time for the big children
and long past it for the little ones
as we turned to go
and the height of the season went by us;

tendrils, leaps, gnarls of blossom,
asteroids and day-stars of our small world,
the sweet-pea ascending the trellis
the clematis descended
while day backed into night
and separate darks blended the shadows,
singling a star out of thin air

as we went in.

Lace

Bent over
the open notebook—

light fades out
making the trees stand out
and my room
at the back
of the house, dark.

In the dusk
I am still
looking for it—
the language that is

lace:

a baroque obligation
at the wrist
of a prince
in a petty court.
Look, just look
at the way he shakes out

the thriftless phrases,
the crystal rhetoric
of bobbined knots
and bosses:
a vagrant drift
of emphasis
to wave away an argument
or frame the hand
he kisses;
which, for all that, is still

what someone
in the corner
of a room;
in the dusk;
bent over
as the light was fading

lost their sight for.

The Bottle Garden

I decanted them—feather mosses, fan-shaped plants,
asymmetric greys in the begonia—
into this globe which shows up how the fern shares
the invertebrate lace of the sea-horse.

The sun is in the bottle garden,
submarine, out of its element
when I come down on a spring morning;
my sweet, greenish, inland underwater.

And in my late thirties, past the middle way,
I can say how did I get here?
I hardly know the way back, still less forward.
Still, if you look for them, there are signs:

Earth stars, rock spleenwort, creeping fig
and English ivy all furled and herded
into the green and cellar wet
of the bottle; well, here they are

here I am a gangling schoolgirl
in the convent library, the April evening outside,
reading the *Aeneid* as the room darkens
to the underworld of the Sixth book—

the Styx, the damned, the pity and
the improvised poetic of imprisoned meanings;
only half aware of the open weave of harbour lights
and my school blouse riding up at the sleeves.

Suburban Woman: A Detail

I

The chimneys have been swept.
The gardens have their winter cut.
The shrubs are prinked, the hedges gelded.

The last dark shows up the headlights
of the cars coming down the Dublin mountains.

Our children used to think they were stars.

II

This is not the season
when the goddess rose
out of seed, out of wheat,
out of thawed water
and went, distracted and astray,
to find her daughter.

Winter will be soon:
Dun pools of rain;
ruddy, addled distances;
winter pinks, tinges and
a first-thing smell of turf
when I take the milk in.

III

Setting out for a neighbour's house
in a denim skirt,

a blouse blended in
by the last light,

I am definite
to start with
but the light is lessening,
the hedge losing its detail,
the path its edge.

Look at me, says the tree.
I was a woman once like you,
full-skirted, human.

Suddenly I am not certain
of the way I came
or the way I will return,
only that something
which may be nothing
more than darkness has begun
softening the definitions
of my body, leaving

the fears and all the terrors
of the flesh shifting the airs
and forms of the autumn quiet

crying "remember us."

The Briar Rose

Intimate as underthings
beside the matronly damasks—

the last thing
to go out at night
is the lantern-like, white insistence
of these small flowers;

their camisole glow.

Standing here on the front step
watching wildness break out again

it could be
the unlighted stairway,
I could be
the child I was, opening

a bedroom door
on Irish whiskey, lipstick,
an empty glass,
oyster crepe-de-Chine

and closing it without knowing why.

The Women

This is the hour I love: the in-between,
neither here-nor-there hour of evening.
The air is tea-colored in the garden.
The briar rose is spilled crepe-de-Chine.

This is the time I do my work best,
going up the stairs in two minds,
in two worlds, carrying cloth or glass,
leaving something behind, bringing
something with me I should have left behind.

The hour of change, of metamorphosis,
of shape-shifting instabilities.
My time of sixth sense and second sight
when in the words I choose, the lines I write,
they rise like visions and appear to me:

women of work, of leisure, of the night,
in stove-colored silks, in lace, in nothing,
with crewel needles, with books, with wide open legs

who fled the hot breath of the god pursuing,
who ran from the split hoof and the thick lips
and fell and grieved and healed into myth,

into me in the evening at my desk
testing the water with a sweet quartet,
the physical force of a dissonance—

the fission of music into syllabic heat—
and getting sick of it and standing up
and going downstairs in the last brightness

into a landscape without emphasis,
light, linear, precisely planned,
a hemisphere of tiered, aired cotton,

a hot terrain of linen from the iron,
folded in and over, stacked high,
neatened flat, stoving heat and white.

Nocturne

After a friend has gone I like the feel of it:
The house at night. Everyone asleep.
The way it draws in like atmosphere or evening.

One-o-clock. A floral teapot and a raisin scone.
A tray waits to be taken down.
The landing light is off. The clock strikes. The cat

comes into his own, mysterious on the stairs,
a black ambivalence around the legs of button-back
chairs, an insinuation to be set beside

the red spoon and the salt-glazed cup,
the saucer with the thick spill of tea
which scalds off easily under the tap. Time

is a tick, a purr, a drop. The spider
on the dining-room window has fallen asleep
among complexities as I will once

the doors are bolted and the keys tested
and the switch turned up of the kitchen light
which made outside in the back garden

an electric room—a domestication
of closed daisies, an architecture
instant and improbable.

The Fire in Our Neighborhood

The sign factory went on fire last night.
Maybe "factory" is too strong a word.
They painted window-signs there when times
were good, wooden battens, glass, plaster-board.

The paint cans went off like rifle fire.
By the time we heard sirens we were standing
at the windows watching ordinary things—
garden walls, pools of rain—reflecting

violent ornamentation,
our world grown elaborate as if
down-to-earth cloth and wood became
gimp and tatting, guipure and japanning.

Familiar figures became curious shadows.
Everyday men and women were the restless
enigmatic shapes behind glass.
Then the sirens stopped; the end began.

It didn't take long. The fire brigade
turned their hoses on the sawmills where
the rock band practices on Saturdays
with the loud out-of-tune bass guitar.

And the flames went out. The night
belonged to the dark again, to the scent
of rain in the air, to its print on the pavement
and the neighbors who slept through the excitement.

On Holiday

Ballyvaughan.
Peat and salt.
How the wind bawls
across the mountains,
scalds the orchids
of the Burren.

They used to leave milk
out once on these windowsills
to ward away
the child-stealing spirits.

The sheets are damp.
We sleep between the blankets.
The light cotton of the curtains
lets the light in.

You wake first thing
and in your five-year-size
striped nightie you are
everywhere trying everything:
the springs on the bed,
the hinges on the window.

You know your a's and b's
but there's a limit now
to what you'll believe.

When dark comes I leave
a superstitious feast
of wheat biscuits, apples,
orange juice out for you
and wake to find it eaten.

Growing Up

(from Renoir's drawing *Girlhood*)

Their two heads, hatted, bowed, mooning
above their waist-high tides of hair
pair hopes.
          This is the haul and full
of fantasy:
          full-skirted girls,
a canvas blued and empty with the view
of unschemed space and the anemic
quick of the pencil picking out
dreams blooding them with womanhood.

They face the future. If they only knew!

There in the distance, bonneted,
round as the hairline of a child—
indefinite and infinite with hope—
is the horizon, is the past and all
they look forward to is memory.

There and Back

Years ago I left the guest-house
in the first September light
with no sense
I would remember this:

starting up the engine
by the river, picking up
speed on the road
signposted Dublin,

measuring Kilkenny, Carlow, Naas
as distances not places,
yearning for my own
version of the world

every small town was
taking down
its shutters to
and I was still miles from;

until I shut the car door sharp
at eight years ago and you were
with the children,
with their bottles,

at your heels, the little radiances
of their faces turned up,
heliotropic,
to our kiss.

The Wild Spray

It came to me one afternoon in summer—
a gift of long-stemmed flowers in a wet
contemporary sheath of newspapers
which pieced off easily at the sink.

I put them in an ironstone jug
near the window; now years later
I know the names for the flowers
they were but not the shape they made:

The true rose beside the mountain rose,
the muslin finery of asparagus fern,
rosemary, forsythia; something about it was
confined and free in the days that followed

which were the brute, final days of summer—
a consistency of milk about the heat haze,
midges freighting the clear space between
the privet and the hedge, the nights chilling

quickly into stars, the morning breaking late
and on the low table the wild spray
lasted for days, a sweet persuasion,
a random guess becoming a definition.

I have remembered it in a certain way—
displayed yellows and the fluencies
of colors in a jug making a statement of
the unfurnished grace of white surfaces

the way I remember us when we first came here
and had no curtains; the lights on the mountain
that winter were sharp, distant promises
like crocuses through the snowfall of darkness.

We stood together at an upstairs window
enchanted by the patterns in the haphazard,
watching the streetlamp making rain into
a planet of tears near the whitebeam trees.

The Journey

(FOR ELIZABETH RYLE)

Immediately cries were heard. These were the loud wailing of infant
souls weeping at the very entrance-way; never had they had their share of
life's sweetness for the dark day had stolen them from their mothers'
breasts and plunged them to a death before their time.
                                        —Virgil, *The Aeneid*, Book VI

And then the dark fell and "there has never,"
I said, "been a poem to an antibiotic:
never a word to compare with the odes on
the flower of the raw sloe for fever

"or the devious Africa-seeking tern
or the protein treasures of the sea-bed.
Depend on it, somewhere a poet is wasting
his sweet uncluttered metres on the obvious

"emblem instead of the real thing.
Instead of sulpha we shall have hyssop dipped
in the wild blood of the unblemished lamb,
so every day the language gets less

"for the task and we are less with the language."
I finished speaking and the anger faded
and dark fell and the book beside me
lay open at the page Aphrodite

comforts Sappho in her love's duress.
The poplars shifted their music in the garden,
a child startled in a dream,
my room was a mess—

the usual hardcovers, half-finished cups,
clothes piled up on an old chair—

and I was listening out but in my head was
a loosening and sweetening heaviness,

not sleep, but nearly sleep, not dreaming really
but as ready to believe and still
unfevered, calm and unsurprised
when she came and stood beside me

and I would have known her anywhere
and I would have gone with her anywhere
and she came wordlessly
and without a word I went with her

down down down without so much as
ever touching down but always, always
with a sense of mulch beneath us,
the way of stairs winding down to a river

and as we went on the light went on
failing and I looked sideways to be certain
it was she, misshapen, musical—
Sappho—the scholiast's nightingale

and down we went, again down
until we came to a sudden rest
beside a river in what seemed to be
an oppressive suburb of the dawn.

My eyes got slowly used to the bad light.
At first I saw shadows, only shadows.
Then I could make out women and children
and, in the way they were, the grace of love.

"Cholera, typhus, croup, diphtheria,"
she said, "in those days they racketed
in every backstreet and alley of old Europe.
Behold the children of the plague."

Then to my horror I could see to each
nipple some had clipped a limpet shape—
suckling darknesses—while others had their arms weighed
down, making terrible pietàs.

She took my sleeve and said to me, "Be careful.
Do not define these women by their work:
not as washerwomen trussed in dust and sweating,
muscling water into linen by the river's edge

"nor as court ladies brailled in silk
on wool and woven with an ivory unicorn
and hung, nor as laundresses tossing cotton,
brisking daylight with lavender and gossip.

"But these are women who went out like you
when dusk became a dark sweet with leaves,
recovering the day, stooping, picking up
teddy bears and rag dolls and tricycles and buckets—

"love's archaeology—and they too like you
stood boot deep in flowers once in summer
or saw winter come in with a single magpie
in a caul of haws, a solo harlequin."

I stood fixed. I could not reach or speak to them.
Between us was the melancholy river,
the dream water, the narcotic crossing
and they had passed over it, its cold persuasions.

I whispered, "Let me be
let me at least be their witness," but she said,
"What you have seen is beyond speech,
beyond song, only not beyond love;

"remember it, you will remember it"
and I heard her say but she was fading fast
as we emerged under the stars of heaven,
"There are not many of us; you are dear

"and stand beside me as my own daughter.
I have brought you here so you will know forever
the silences in which are our beginnings,
in which we have an origin like water,"

and the wind shifted and the window clasp
opened, banged and I woke up to find

the poetry books stacked higgledy- piggledy,
my skirt spread out where I had laid it—

nothing was changed; nothing was more clear
but it was wet and the year was late.
The rain was grief in arrears; my children
slept the last dark out safely and I wept.

Envoi

It is Easter in the suburb. Clematis
shrubs the eaves and trellises with pastel.
The evenings lengthen and before the rain
the Dublin mountains become visible.

My muse must be better than those of men
who made theirs in the image of their myth.
The work is half-finished and I have nothing.
but the crudest measures to complete it with.

Under the street-lamps the dustbins brighten.
The winter flowering jasmine casts a shadow
outside my window in my neighbor's garden.
These are the things that my muse must know.

She must come to me. Let her come
to be among the donnée, the given.
I need her to remain with me until
the day is over and the song is proven.

Surely she comes, surely she comes to me—
no lizard skin, no paps, no podded womb
about her but a brightening and
the consequences of an April tomb.

What I have done I have done alone.
What I have seen is unverified.
I have the truth and I need the faith.
It is time I put my hand in her side.

If she will not bless the ordinary,
if she will not sanctify the common,
then here I am and here I stay and then am I
the most miserable of women.

Listen. This Is the Noise of Myth

This is the story of a man and woman
under a willow and beside a weir
near a river in a wooded clearing.
They are fugitives. Intimates of myth.

Fictions of my purpose. I suppose
I shouldn't say that yet or at least
before I break their hearts or save their lives
I ought to tell their story and I will.

When they went first it was winter; cold,
cold through the Midlands and as far West
as they could go. They knew they had to go—
through Meath, Westmeath, Longford,

their lives unraveling like the hours of light—
and then there were lambs under the snow
and it was January, aconite and jasmine
and the hazel yellowing and puce berries on the ivy.

They could not eat where they had cooked,
nor sleep where they had eaten
nor at dawn rest where they had slept.
They shunned the densities

of trees with one trunk and of caves
with one dark and the dangerous embrace
of islands with a single landing place.
And all the time it was cold, cold:

the fields still gardened by their ice,
the trees stitched with snow overnight,
the ditches full; frost toughening lichen,
darning lace into rock crevices.

And then the woods flooded and buds
blunted from the chestnut and the foxglove
put its big leaves out and chaffinches
chinked and flirted in the branches of the ash.

And here we are where we started from—
under a willow and beside a weir
near a river in a wooded clearing.
The woman and the man have come to rest.

Look how light is coming through the ash.
The weir sluices kingfisher blues.
The woman and the willow tree lean forward, forward.
Something is near; something is about to happen;

something more than spring
and less than history. Will we see
hungers eased after months of hiding?
Is there a touch of heat in that light?

If they stay here soon it will be summer; things
returning, sunlight fingering minnowy deeps,
seedy greens, reeds, electing lights
and edges from the river. Consider

legend, self-deception, sin, the sum
of human purpose and its end; remember
how our poetry depends on distance,
aspect: gravity will bend starlight.

Forgive me if I set the truth to rights.
Bear with me if I put an end to this:
She never turned to him; she never leaned
under the sallow-willow over to him.

They never made love; not there; not here;
not anywhere; there was no winter journey;
no aconite, no birdsong and no jasmine,
no woodland and no river and no weir.

Listen. This is the noise of myth. It makes
the same sound as shadow. Can you hear it?

Daylight grays in the preceptories.
Her head begins to shine

pivoting the planets of a harsh nativity.
They were never mine. This is mine.
This sequence of evicted possibilities.
Displaced facts. Tricks of light. Reflections.

Invention. Legend. Myth. What you will.
The shifts and fluencies are infinite.
The moving parts are marvelous. Consider
how the bereavements of the definite

are easily lifted from our heroine.
She may or she may not. She was or wasn't
by the water at his side as dark
waited above the Western countryside.

O consolations of the craft.
How we put
the old poultices on the old sores,
the same mirrors to the old magic. Look.

The scene returns. The willow sees itself
drowning in the weir and the woman
gives the kiss of myth her human heat.
Reflections. Reflections. He becomes her lover.

The old romances make no bones about it.
The long and short of it. The end and the beginning.
The glories and the ornaments are muted.
And when the story ends the song is over.

An Irish Childhood in England: 1951

The bickering of vowels on the buses,
the clicking thumbs and the big hips of
the navy-skirted ticket collectors with
their crooked seams brought it home to me:
Exile. Ration-book pudding.
Bowls of dripping and the fixed smile
of the school pianist playing "Iolanthe,"
"Land of Hope and Glory"
and "John Peel."

I didn't know what to hold, to keep.
At night, filled with some malaise
of love for what I'd never known I had,
I fell asleep and let the moment pass.
The passing moment has become a night
of clipped shadows, freshly painted houses,
the garden eddying in dark and heat,
my children half-awake, half-asleep.

Airless, humid dark. Leaf-noise.
The stirrings of a garden before rain.
A hint of storm behind the risen moon.
We are what we have chosen. Did I choose to?—
in a strange city, in another country,
on nights in a North-facing bedroom,
waiting for the sleep that never did
restore me as I'd hoped to what I'd lost—

let the world I knew become the space
between the words that I had by heart
and all the other speech that always was
becoming the language of the country that
I came to in nineteen-fifty-one:
barely-gelled, a freckled six-year-old,

overdressed and sick on the plane
when all of England to an Irish child

was nothing more than what you'd lost and how:
was the teacher in the London convent who
when I produced "I amn't" in the classroom
turned and said—"you're not in Ireland now."

Fond Memory

It was a school where all the children wore darned worsted;
where they cried—or almost all—when the Reverend Mother
announced at lunch-time that the King had died

peacefully in his sleep. I dressed in wool as well,
ate rationed food, played English games and learned
how wise the Magna Carta was, how hard the Hanoverians

had tried, the measure and complexity of verse,
the hum and score of the whole orchestra.
At three-o-clock I caught two buses home

where sometimes in the late afternoon
at a piano pushed into a corner of the playroom
my father would sit down and play the slow

lilts of Tom Moore while I stood there trying
not to weep at the cigarette smoke stinging up
from between his fingers and—as much as I could think—

I thought this is my country, was, will be again,
this upward-straining song made to be
our safe inventory of pain. And I was wrong.

Canaletto in the National Gallery of Ireland

Something beating in
making pain and attention—
a heat still
livid on the skin
is the might-have-been:

the nation, the city
which fell
for want of
the elevation in
this view of the Piazza,

its everyday light
making it everyone's
remembered city:
airs and shadows,
cambered distances.

I remember
a city like this—
the static coral
of reflected brick
in its river.

I envy these
pin-pointed citizens
their solid ease,
their lack of any need
to come and see

the beloved republic
raised
and saved
and scalded into
something measurable.

The Emigrant Irish

Like oil lamps we put them out the back,

of our houses, of our minds. We had lights
better than, newer than and then

a time came, this time and now
we need them. Their dread, makeshift example.

They would have thrived on our necessities.
What they survived we could not even live.
By their lights now it is time to
imagine how they stood there, what they stood with,
that their possessions may become our power.

Cardboard. Iron. Their hardships parceled in them.
Patience. Fortitude. Long-suffering
in the bruise-colored dusk of the New World.

And all the old songs. And nothing to lose.

Tirade for the Lyric Muse

You're propped and swabbed and bedded.
I could weep.
There's a stench of snipped flesh
and tubed blood.
I've come to see if beauty is skin deep.

Mongrel features.
Tainted lint and cotton.
Sutures from the lip to ear to brow.
They've patched your wrinkles
and replaced your youth.
It may be beauty
but it isn't truth.

You are the victim of a perfect crime.
You have no sense of time.
You never had.
You never dreamed he could be so cruel.
Which is why you lie back
shocked in cambric,
slacked in bandages
and blubbing gruel.
My white python writhing your renewal!

I loved you once.
It seemed so right, so neat.
The moon, the month, the flower, the kiss—
there wasn't anything that wouldn't fit.
The ends were easy
and the means were short
when you and I were lyric and elect.
Shall I tell you what we overlooked?

You in this bed.
You with your snout,

your seams, your stitches
and your sutured youth.
You,
you with your smocked mouth
are what your songs left out.

We still have time.
Look in the glass.
Time is the flaw.
Truth is the crystal.

We have been sisters
in the crime.
Let us be sisters
in the physic:

Listen.
Bend your darned head.
Turn your good ear.
Share my music.

The Woman Takes Her Revenge on the Moon

Claret. Plum. Cinnabar.
The damask of the peach.
The flame and sweet
carmine of late berries.
The orchard colors of the morning—

I am learning them.
I streak ochers on my cheeks.
This is my makeup box.
This is how I own
the tone secrets of the dawn.

It takes skill
to make my skin
a facsimile
of absolute light,
of scarlet turning into carmine.

Once I start
I lose all sense
of time, of space,
of clarity, of will.
I mix to kill.

Orange madder.
The magenta tint.
I am perfecting it.
It must be excellent
or she won't fall for it.

I fresh the pearly wet
across my face.
I rouge the flesh.
I spread and flush the red.
The trap is set.

I walk out
in the evening air.
Early, early
in the clear evening.
I raise my head like a snare.

There it is.
I can feel it—
the pleasure of it!—
the dun slither,
the hysteric of her white

expression, its surprise
as she drowns,
as she douses
in my face,
in my sunrise.

The Glass King

Isabella of Bavaria married Charles VI of France in 1385. In later years
his madness took the form of believing he was made from glass.

When he is ready he is raised and carried
among his vaporish plants; the palms and ferns flex;
they almost bend; you'd almost think they were going to kiss him;
and so they might; but she will not, his wife,

no she can't kiss his lips in case he splinters
into a million Bourbons, mad pieces.
What can she do with him—her daft prince?
His nightmares are the Regency of France.

Yes, she's been through it all, his Bavaroise,
blub-hipped and docile, urgent to be needed—
from churching to milk fever, from tongue-tied princess
to the queen of a mulish king—and now this.

They were each other's fantasy in youth.
No splintering at all about that mouth
when they were flesh and muscle, woman and man,
fire and kindling. See that silk divan?

Enough said. Now the times themselves
are his asylum: these are the Middle Ages, sweet
and savage era of the saving grace; indulgences
are two a penny; under the stonesmith's hand

stone turns into lace. I need his hand now.
Outside my window October soaks the stone;
you can hear it; you'd almost think
the brick was drinking it; the rowan drips

and history waits. Let it wait. I want
no elsewheres: the clover-smelling, stove-warm

air of autumn catches cold; the year turns;
the leaves fall; the poem hesitates:

If we could see ourselves, not as we do—
in mirrors, self-deceptions, self-regardings—
but as we ought to be and as we have been:
poets, lute-stringers, makyres and abettors

of our necessary art, soothsayers of the ailment
and disease of our times, sweet singers,
truth tellers, intercessors for self-knowledge—
what would we think of these fin-de-siècle

half-hearted penitents we have become
at the sick-bed of the century: hand-wringing
elegists with an ill-concealed greed
for the inheritance?
                    My prince, demented

in a crystal past, a lost France, I elect you emblem
and ancestor of our lyric: it fits you like a glove—
doesn't it?—the part; untouchable, outlandish,
esoteric, inarticulate and out of reach

of human love: studied every day by your wife,
an ordinary honest woman out of place
in all this, wanting nothing more than the man
she married, all her sorrows in her stolid face.

Index